Music Through Children's Literature

MUSIC THROUGH CHILDREN'S LITERATURE
Theme and Variations
Revised Edition

Donna B. Levene

Illustrations by Susan Kochenberger Stroeher

2001

TEACHER IDEAS PRESS
A Division of
Libraries Unlimited, Inc.
Englewood, Colorado

Dedicated to my family, Barry, Nathan, and Alex,
for their encouragement and patience
and to my mother, Emily Borchardt
who kept me on track by beginning each telephone conversation with
"How much more have you written?"

TEACHER IDEAS PRESS
A Division of
Libraries Unlimited, Inc.
P.O. Box 6633
Englewood, CO 80155-6633
www.lu.com/tip

Library of Congress Cataloging-in-Publication Data for First Edition

Levene, Donna B.
　　Music through children's literature : theme and variations / Donna
B. Levene ; illustrations by Susan Kochenberger Stroeher.
　　viii, 117 p. 22x28 cm.
　　Includes bibliographical references, discographies, and index.
　　ISBN 1-56308-021-4
　　1. Music--Instruction and study--Juvenile. 2. Music appreciation.
I. Title.
MT10.L55 1993
372.87--dc20
　　　　　　　　　　　　　　　　　　　　　　　93-22070
　　　　　　　　　　　　　　　　　　　　　　　CIP
　　　　　　　　　　　　　　　　　　　　　　　MN

CONTENTS

Preface to Revised Edition vii
Preface to First Edition ix

RHYTHM

Chicka Chicka Boom Boom (B. Martin, Jr., and Archambault) 3
The Completed Hickory Dickory Dock (Aylesworth) 5
Crocodile Beat (Jorgensen) 8
Miss Mary Mack: And Other Children's Street Rhymes (Cole and Calmenson) 10
Possum Come A-Knockin' (Van Laan) 12
Train Song (Siebert) 15

MELODY

All the Pretty Horses (Jeffers) 21
Fiddle-I-Fee: A Farmyard Song for the Very Young (Sweet) 23
Georgia Music (Griffith) 25
Grandma's Band (Bowles) 28
Mary Wore Her Red Dress, and Henry Wore His Green Sneakers (Peek) 30
Sing, Pierrot, Sing: A Picture Book in Mime (dePaola) 32
Ten Bears in My Bed: A Goodnight Countdown (Mack) 34
There's a Hole in the Bucket (Westcott) 37

FORM & STYLE

Bonjour, Mr. Satie (dePaola) 41
The Complete Story of the Three Blind Mice (Ivimey) 44
Joyful Noise: Poems for Two Voices (Fleischman) 46
Mama Don't Allow (Hurd) 48
Nathaniel Talking (Greenfield) 51
Rondo in C (Fleischman) 54

INSTRUMENTS

All Join In (Blake) 59
Berlioz the Bear (Brett) 61
City Sounds (Emberley) 64
Good Times on Grandfather Mountain (Martin) 66
Music, Music for Everyone (Williams) 68
Nicholas Cricket (Maxner) 70
Oh, A-Hunting We Will Go (Langstaff) 72

DANCES

Barn Dance (B. Martin, Jr., and Archambault)......................77
The Dancing Granny (Bryan)......................79
Dancing the Breeze (Shannon)......................81
Dinosaur Dances (Yolen)......................83
Mirandy and Brother Wind (McKissack)......................86
Shimmy Shake Earthquake: Don't Forget to Dance Poems (Jabar)......................88
Skip to My Lou (Westcott)......................90

HISTORY

The Boy Who Loved Music (Lasker)......................95
Cowboy Dreams (Khalsa)......................98
The Erie Canal (Spier)......................101
Follow the Drinking Gourd (Winter)......................103
Mozart Tonight (Downing)......................105
Ragtime Tumpie (Schroeder)......................107

Song Collections......................111

Annotated Bibliography Supplement......................113

Index......................127

About the Author......................131

PREFACE TO REVISED EDITION

Music is alive in children's books! There is rhythm in Max's two sticks pounding on a garbage can lid, melody in the folk tune "Jennie Jenkins," and dances at the reptile ball. The blues come to life on a "low-down laundry line," a family celebrates song with a Saturday night jamboree, and the "Zebra-riding cowboy" rides into the sunset on a dotted rhythm. Since the publication of *Music Through Children's Literature: Theme and Variations* in 1993, children's authors and illustrators have created a wide variety of excellent new books that can foster a child's delight in music.

The annotated bibliography supplement included in this new edition is intended to expand the range of choices in teaching the lessons in this book. Many of the books, songbooks, and recordings are still available in public and school library collections. However, if they are not, alternative books that will teach the same musical concept are suggested. In addition, some books have been added that will provide teachers with options for expanding the focus of the lesson.

In the first edition, the references to recordings were limited to audiocassette tapes. I have expanded the materials in the supplement to include CDs. Many music books are now published with accompanying CDs, a practice that provides an ideal marriage of text, illustration, and sound for classroom or library presentations.

The Internet has made access to books and music easier and faster; there are two Internet sites that I would highly recommend for folk or jazz music. Teachers will find these helpful in their own searches for music. Each of these sites contains audio excerpts of music.

The Web site at *http://www.pbs.org/jazz* contains biographies, jazz lessons that include musical excerpts, and many other helpful links to jazz information. This site was created to complement the PBS series, *Jazz: A Film by Ken Burns*. The series has also spawned a host of jazz CD remakes, one of which is included in the bibliography.

The Web site at *http://web2.si.edu/folkways/dbstart.htm* contains a database of recordings searchable by artist/performer, recording title, and track title. The Smithsonian Institution acquired Folkways Records in 1987. Under the label Smithsonian Folkways Recordings, more than 2,000 of Folkways historic folk music recordings have been reissued.

I am encouraged by the quality and quantity of resources available for teaching music to children. The supplement provides teachers with more of these tools to connect literature and music, as the rhythmic and lyrical qualities of the texts mirror the meter and melody of the song. Making these connections for children can only increase their sense of wonder for the music that surrounds them.

PREFACE TO FIRST EDITION

Leonard Bernstein, American composer and conductor, once described music as "heightened speech."[1] When words can no longer express the message or emotion, pitched sound takes over. Music is everywhere—not only in concert halls and compact disc players, but in the sounds of the night, the rhythm of a train, and the singsong chants of children. It permeates our lives but is often unnoticed.

However, children seem attuned to sound and respond to music, often humming, tapping, or dancing to its rhythms. Drawing on his own childhood experience, Maurice Sendak, noted author of literature for all ages, described the role music played in his early life: "Music's peculiar power of releasing fantasy has always fascinated me. An inseparable part of my memories of childhood, music was the inevitable animating accompaniment to the make-believe."[2]

This book, incorporating musical variations on a literature theme, brings together a child's musical leanings with literature that has musical qualities. Each lesson is based on a children's book. In some, the musical connection is evident: the books include illustrated folk songs or explanations of a style or form in musical history. Others are inherently musical in the lyricism of the authors' words or the rhythm of the text. As Paul Fleischman noted in his Newbery acceptance speech for *Joyful Noise: Poems for Two Voices*, "Writing prose has much in common with writing music.... Every chapter, every paragraph, every sentence, I discovered, has an arc to it, like a musical phrase. Every word has both a meaning and a music."[3]

I have divided the book into six sections: "Rhythm," "Melody," "Form & Style," "Instruments," "Dances," "History." This grouping allows teachers to emphasize specific concepts and to concentrate on their musical strengths. If you like to sing, select lessons from the "Melody" section. If you enjoy movement activities, choose the "Dance" section.

The degree of musical aptitude required to teach the lessons varies within each section so that there is generally at least one activity that will match the teacher's skills and experience level. Also, the lessons are flexible enough that some elements can be omitted.

This book is written for teachers who enjoy music and would like to incorporate it into their literature or social studies units. It can be used by collaborative teams of classroom teachers and music specialists, or media and music specialists. Because each lesson is self-contained, the book can also be used successfully by public librarians for story time or as a resource by substitute music teachers.

The structure of the lessons within each section is patterned after the musical structure of a sonata movement written in sonata form. Often called the sonata-allegro form, it consists of an exposition, development, recapitulation, and, occasionally, coda. These sections of the movement are analogous to the major divisions of a lesson plan.

In the sonata form, the exposition states the main musical themes. In a teaching lesson, the "Exposition" constitutes the beginning of the lesson, in which the teacher states the objectives and prepares the students for the activity. Sometimes referred to as the anticipatory set, this is the time when the students' curiosity is captured and the schema is activated.

The development follows. This section develops and explores the themes that were introduced in the exposition. Bernstein described this section of a sonata movement as "startling new looks at old material."[4] At this point in the lesson, the students participate in discussion or activities that expand their knowledge of the themes of the book. The teacher and students try out these activities together. The "Development" is the practice session.

In a sonata movement, the recapitulation is a restatement of the original musical themes. This corresponds to the closure section of a lesson. Students demonstrate what they have learned by drawing conclusions about the book and performing a task related to the theme. The products are often accomplished by collaborative groups.

The movement could end here, but often a coda is added. The coda, or "tail," is a passage that gives the piece of music a definite ending. The composer is saying, "one more time, with feeling." The "Coda" in the lesson presents extended activities that expand the length and focus of the lesson. Often these ideas develop into performance outlets.

The "Exposition," "Development," "Recapitulation," and "Coda" are preceded in the lesson plans by the theme, which states the purpose of the lesson; a list of resources; a discography; and a list of keywords, which defines terms introduced in the theme or likely to be encountered during the lesson.

I have tried to cite resources that are readily available in school and public libraries. Some of the song collections are out of print but are still housed in library collections. As you plan a lesson, consult with your school library media specialist or public librarian. Their expertise in locating materials can be invaluable.

In compiling the discographies, I have included cassette tapes that are listed either in the recent issue of *Opus: America's Guide to Classical Music* or *Phonolog*, so they should be available at local record stores. I have listed only cassette tapes because they are the format most accessible to schools. The best resource for music tapes is the music teacher. However, don't overlook the avocations of family, friends, parents, and other staff members. Someone you know may have a comprehensive tape collection. Most of the pieces listed are well known and available on a variety of labels.

I hope this book serves a practical purpose by providing teachers with a vehicle for enhancing and encouraging children's natural affinity for music. Sing a familiar tune or pull out a tambourine, and children respond. Start a rhythmic beat, and children move. Both music and books should be integral parts of a child's life. Presenting them in tandem will bring us closer to "heightened speech."

I would like to thank my friends and colleagues who freely shared their teaching and musical expertise by offering helpful advice on content and provided the support to keep me continually challenged. My editor, Suzanne Barchers, encouraged me to begin this project and bolstered my confidence throughout. Neysa Lettin read the manuscript from a music teacher's viewpoint and supported the idea of collaborative teaching. Susan Stroeher, kindergarten teacher by trade and artist by nature, read all the books and lessons and produced such whimsical, comical drawings that the book would seem incomplete without them. Finally, thanks to my friends in Delta Omicron International Music Fraternity who were an enthusiastic audience for my booktalk/recital that was the impetus for the ideas in this book.

NOTES

[1]Leonard Bernstein, *The Unanswered Question: Six Talks at Harvard*, the Charles Eliot Norton Lectures, 1973 (Cambridge, Mass.: Harvard University Press, 1976), 15.

[2]Maurice Sendak, *Caldecott & Co.: Notes on Books & Pictures*, Michael de Capua Books (New York: Farrar, Straus & Giroux, 1988), 4.

[3]Paul Fleischman, "Newbery Medal Acceptance," *Horn Book Magazine* 65 (July/August 1989): 442-451.

[4]Bernstein, 43.

Rhythm

Chicka Chicka Boom Boom by Bill Martin, Jr., and John Archambault

The Completed Hickory Dickory Dock by Jim Aylesworth

Crocodile Beat by Gail Jorgensen

Miss Mary Mack: And Other Children's Street Rhymes compiled by Joanna Cole and Stephanie Calmenson

Possum Come A-Knockin' by Nancy Van Laan

Train Song by Diane Siebert

CHICKA CHICKA BOOM BOOM

By Bill Martin, Jr., and John Archambault.
Illustrated by Lois Ehlert.
New York: Simon & Schuster, 1989.

A rhyming alphabet climbs up a coconut tree in colorful lowercase letters. "Chicka Chicka Boom Boom. Will there be enough room?"

Lesson grade level: Pre-K to 3

THEME

Combining the nonsense syllables of cheers with the vocal improvisation of scat singing, students will perform *Chicka Chicka Boom Boom* with cheers and a rhythm section.

RESOURCES

Kliment, Bud. *Ella Fitzgerald*. New York: Chelsea House, 1988.

This extensive biography includes a bibliography and a discography.

McKissack, Patricia, and Frederick McKissack. *Louis Armstrong: Jazz Musician*. Illustrated by Ned O. Great African American Series. Hillside, N.J.: Enslow, 1991.

This easily read biography mentions Armstrong's use of scat singing to imitate his trumpet.

DISCOGRAPHY

Armstrong, Louis. *The Legendary Louis Armstrong*. CBS Records, 1990. BT 21727. Sound cassette.

Chicka Chicka Boom Boom. Ray Charles, John Archambault. Simon & Schuster, 1991. Sound cassette.

Ellis, Shirley. "The Name Game." MCA Records, originally released as KJB-70 in 1966. MCA-60024. Sound recording.

KEYWORDS

Cheer — a set of words written to elicit enthusiasm and encouragement from a crowd.

Improvisation — method of inventing the music during the performance.

Pitch — the highness or lowness of musical tones.

Scat singing — a jazz vocal style in which the vocalist uses nonsense syllables to improvise a melody line in imitation of an instrument.

EXPOSITION

1. Lead the students in a cheer: "Give me a *B*! (B) Give me an *O*! (O) Give me another *O*! (O) Give me an *M*! (M) What does that spell? (Boom) I can't hear you! (Boom!) Chicka chicka boom boom. Will there be enough room? Let's hear it for Miss Murphy's room." (Using pom-poms would be very effective.)

2. Talk about other cheers the students may know (rah rah sis boom bah) and the origin of cheers. Discuss the use of nonsense syllables in cheers. Why is this done?

3. Show the cover of *Chicka Chicka Boom Boom* and explain that John Archambault got the idea for this book from hearing a cheer for reading.

DEVELOPMENT

1. Play the tape of Ray Charles reading the book as you show the students the pictures. Ask them to join in on the "chicka chicka...."

2. Discuss the difference between the letters for the children (lowercase) and the adults (uppercase).

3. Teach the students the section "skit skat...." Try it with different pitches, ascending and descending. Have the students mimic you. Mention that some jazz singers improvise melodies using nonsense syllables and that this is called *scat singing*. It probably originated with Louis Armstrong's imitating his trumpet's melodic line. If available, play a recording by Ella Fitzgerald or Louis Armstrong. (Ellis's "The Name Game" plays with names by substituting different beginning sounds to produce a rhythmic nonsense song.)

4. Play the part of the tape that has the rhythmic accompaniment and ask the students to keep the beat by snapping their fingers or patting their legs.

5. Ask them to say the words along with the tape. Show the pages in the book for reinforcement.

RECAPITULATION

1. Tell the students that the class is going to work up an arrangement of the book, complete with rhythm instruments and a cheerleading chorus.

2. Assign lines from the book to groups of two or three. The cheerleading chorus will practice the "chicka chicka boom boom" and the "skit skat...." Give the rhythm section some rhythm instruments and encourage them to snap, clap, and so on.

3. As a class, make up some cheers as an introduction and ending. (You could use these cheers to teach spelling words.)

4. Have each student draw some of the letters or trace cutout letters on a sheet of paper. These can be held up as the letters are mentioned. For younger students give each one a cutout letter to decorate and add to a paper coconut tree on the wall.

5. Perform for other classes, possibly starting with a cheer for the teacher.

CODA

1. Have the book and tape available at a center so that small groups can practice learning the words.

2. Teach the students Ellis's "The Name Game," substituting the students' names into the song.

THE COMPLETED HICKORY DICKORY DOCK

By Jim Aylesworth.
Illustrated by Eileen Christelow.
New York: Atheneum, 1990.

Aylesworth follows a mouse through the day, with a verse for each hour, beginning with the familiar "the clock struck one, and down he run."

Lesson grade level: Pre-K to 3

THEME

The students will experience compound duple meter by singing "Hickory Dickory Dock," which is written in 6/8 meter. The verse is also similar to the limerick pattern.

RESOURCES

"Hickory Dickory Dock." In *The Mother Goose Songbook*, (compiled by) Tom Glazer, illustrated by David McPhail, 16-17. New York: Doubleday, 1990.

"Hickory Dickory Dock." In *Singing Bee! A Collection of Favorite Children's Songs*, compiled by Jane Hart, pictures by Anita Lobel, 51. New York: Lothrop, Lee & Shepard Books, 1982.

Livingston, Myra Cohn. *Poem-Making: Ways to Begin Writing Poetry*, 117-125. New York: Harper-Collins, 1991.

Livingston defines a limerick as a five-line poem with lines 1, 2, and 5 rhyming and containing three feet each, and lines 3 and 4 rhyming, with two feet each. She stresses the importance of the anapestic foot, that is, two unaccented syllables followed by an accented syllable.

Lobel, Arnold. *The Book of Pigericks*. New York: Random House, 1984.

This limerick book is all about pigs in different places.

"The Mulberry Bush." In *Singing Bee! A Collection of Favorite Children's Songs*, 80.

KEYWORDS

Compound duple meter — a duple meter multiplied by three, for example, 6/8 (3 x 2/8).

Duple meter — meter with two beats in a measure, for example, 2/8.

Limerick — a verse of five lines in which lines 1, 2, and 5 have three feet or beats, and lines 3 and 4 have two feet or beats. The line pattern is the same for the rhymes.

Meter — the arrangement of beats into groups of equal size with a defined pattern of accented and unaccented beats.

EXPOSITION

1. Ask the students to recite "Hickory Dickory Dock" and then clap for each sound in "hickory" and "dickory." Each word has three sounds.

2. Ask them to name other words that have three sounds, or syllables.

3. Repeat the rhyme again, clapping on the strong beats. Determine that between the strong beats there are sometimes one and sometimes two sounds.

4. Help the students determine that if there is one sound in between, it is no longer an even rhythm. The strong beat is longer, and the rhythm becomes quick slow.

DEVELOPMENT

1. Read *The Completed Hickory Dickory Dock*. Occasionally stop and ask the students to tell you which words have three sounds.

2. At the end of the story, list the first lines on chart paper next to a drawing of a clock with the hour that matches.

3. Let the students choose which verses they want to sing.

4. Have one group of students emphasize the strong beats by saying "tick tock" for each line while the rest of the class is singing the verse. For example:

> Hickory Dickory Dock
>
> (tick   tock   tick   tock)
>
> The mouse ran up the clock
>
> (tick   tock tick   tock)
>
> The clock struck one
>
> (tick   tock)
>
> And down he run
>
> (tick   tock)
>
> Hickory dickory dock
>
> (tick   tock   tick   tock)

5. Ask the students which lines rhyme. Lines 1, 2, and 5 have the same rhyme pattern, and lines 3 and 4 have a different one. With the older students point out that this is the rhyme scheme for a limerick. Discuss why this isn't a true limerick (in the song, there are four beats in lines 1, 2, and 5 instead of three, and the strong beat is on the first syllable in lines 1 and 5 rather than the second).

RECAPITULATION

1. Practice the song as a whole group using the well-known first verse.

2. Once the melody is known, assign verses to groups of four. Because of limited class size, you may need to have each group learn two verses, or limit the assignment to six verses.

3. As each group sings a verse, have the rest of the class chant the "tick tock...." Give a couple of students tone blocks to keep the rhythm even.

4. For more practice with the 6/8 meter, teach the students "The Mulberry Bush."

5. Because the uneven rhythm lends itself to skipping, have the students skip to the right and left as they go 'round the mulberry bush. On the rest of the verses, have them do the actions.

CODA

1. Investigate some limericks if the students are older. Despite the shift in the placement of the accented syllables, the uneven rhythm pattern points out the lilt of compound duple meter.

2. Use Livingston's book to explain the limerick pattern.

3. Using Lobel's *Pigericks* have groups of students choose one of the pigericks to chant, accompanying themselves on rhythm instruments.

CROCODILE BEAT

By Gail Jorgensen.
Illustrated by Patricia Mullins.
New York: Bradbury Press, 1989.

In this rhythmic verse, the crocodile awaits his prey as the jungle animals approach the waterhole in onomatopoeic fashion.

Lesson grade level: 2 and up

THEME

The students will keep a steady beat as they imitate the animal sounds in 4/4 meter.

RESOURCES

Carroll, Lewis. "Crocodile." In *The Random House Book of Poetry for Children*, selected and introduced by Jack Prelutsky, illustrated by Arnold Lobel, 81. New York: Random House, 1983.

This two-stanza poem describes the crocodile's "grin" as he "welcomes little fishes in."

Fleming, Denise. *In the Tall, Tall Grass*. New York: Henry Holt, 1991.

Each two-page spread describes an animal or insect in the tall grass as it moves or eats from lunch to sundown.

Livingston, Myra Cohn. *Poem-Making: Ways to Begin Writing Poetry*, 72-79. New York: Harper-Collins, 1991.

Livingston describes the poetic foot *trochee* using Robert Louis Stevenson's poem "Hiawatha."

Steig, Jeanne. "The Crocodile." In *Consider the Lemming*, pictures by William Steig. New York: Farrar, Straus & Giroux, 1988.

This humorous poem describes the crocodile's grin and appetite.

KEYWORDS

Beats — units used to measure musical time.

Common meter — another name for 4/4 meter, which has four beats in a measure, with the quarter note receiving one beat.

Measure — in musical notation a group of musical beats separated by bar lines.

Meter — the arrangement of beats into groups of equal size with a defined pattern of accented and unaccented beats.

Metronome — a mechanical, electric, or electronic device for sounding a steady beat at various speeds.

Onomatopoeia — the formation of words that imitate or reproduce sound.

Trochee — a foot in poetic meter consisting of two syllables, the first accented and the second unaccented.

EXPOSITION

1. Show the cover of *Crocodile Beat* and ask the students to define a beat. Using a heartbeat as an example, talk about an evenly divided pulse.

2. Demonstrate a metronome and explain that the numbers signify how many beats it counts per minute. Ask the students to match the metronome beats by patting their legs. Try various speeds.

DEVELOPMENT

1. As you read *Crocodile Beat*, ask each student to keep the beat by tapping the left palm with two fingers of the right hand.

2. Read the book as rhythmically as possible. If you have to pause to turn a page, let four beats elapse.

3. At the end of the book, ask the students whether they know how many beats were in each line. Read some pages again to discover that there were four beats.

4. On chart paper write a few lines of the onomatopoeic animal sounds from the book, delineating the poetic measures with bar lines, as in a measure of music. Place a slash mark above the accented words.

5. List the rest of the animal sounds on chart paper and discuss the relationship between the sound of the word and the actual sound made by the animals. Define *onomatopoeia*.

RECAPITULATION

1. Divide the class into nine groups, one for each of the eight animals and one for a rhythm section.

2. Ask the animal groups to use their voices to exaggerate the onomatopoeic sounds. After the groups have practiced, check to see whether they can say the sounds with a steady beat.

3. The rhythm section must decide how it wants to keep the beat going throughout the book. Give members suggestions such as clapping or snapping.

4. Have the rhythm section start and set the beat. Read the book again, with each animal group joining in. The crocodile group can say the "Oh dear!" at the end, and everyone can say "Bye-bye."

5. Once everyone feels comfortable with the sounds, add movement as each group approaches the "river" (the river can be a designated spot in the middle of the area where this activity is taking place).

CODA

1. For a more elaborate production, ask the students to transfer the onomatopoeic animal sounds to rhythm instruments. Members of the rhythm section can add drums to their body rhythms.

2. *In the Tall, Tall Grass* is also written in 4/4 meter and is a perfect complement to *Crocodile Beat* because it describes the sounds of animal and insect movements.

3. Discuss 4/4 meter, or common meter, and relate it to the poetic meter of Stevenson's "Hiawatha." The trochaic foot in this poem corresponds to a beat, and each line has four beats. (See Livingston's *Poem-Making*.)

4. Compare the crocodile poems by Carroll and Steig. The vocabulary is difficult, but here's a chance to learn some new words.

MISS MARY MACK: AND OTHER CHILDREN'S STREET RHYMES

Compiled by Joanna Cole and Stephanie Calmenson.
Illustrated by Alan Tiegreen.
New York: Morrow Junior Books, 1990.

This compilation of American street rhymes offers many opportunities for rhythm and rhyme activities, as well as songs.

Lesson grade level: 2 and up

THEME

Whether clapping, bouncing a ball, or passing a ball in a circle, students will keep the beat while reciting the street rhymes.

RESOURCES

Bayer, Jane. *A My Name Is Alice.* Pictures by Steven Kellogg. New York: Dial Books for Young Readers, 1984.

In this rhythmic alphabet book, the husband's name, the city, and the food the characters eat all begin with the same letter.

Jenkins, Ella. "Mary Mack." In *Holt Music* (Grade 2), (compiled by) Eunice Boardman *et al.*, 28-29. New York: Holt, Rinehart & Winston, 1988.

Jenkins's melodic version of "Mary Mack" is in a minor key and features a descending musical pattern on "down her back."

"Mary Mack." In *Shake It to the One That You Love the Best: Play Songs and Lullabies from Black Musical Traditions*, collected and adapted by Cheryl Warren Mattox, with illustrations from the works of Varnette P. Honeywood and Brenda Joysmith, 15. El Sobrante, Calif.: Warren-Mattox Productions, 1989.

This version differs melodically from Jenkins's but has the same melody as the *Fireside* version (below).

"Miss Mary Mack." In *The Fireside Book of Fun and Games Songs*, collected and edited by Marie Winn, musical arrangements by Allan Miller, illustrations by Whitney Darrow, Jr., 57. New York: Simon & Schuster, 1974.

This version includes a hand-clapping pattern and additional verses for Miss Betty Bean, Miss Lucy Light, Miss Dora Down, and Miss Flora Fay.

DISCOGRAPHY

Mattox, Cheryl Warren, comp. *Shake It to the One That You Love the Best: Play Songs and Lullabies from Black Musical Traditions*. Warren-Mattox Productions. JM 20581. Sound cassette.

EXPOSITION

1. Chant the words of "A My Name Is Alice" and follow the ball-bouncing instructions on page 26 of *Miss Mary Mack*. Do as many verses as you can memorize.

2. Ask the students to show you any ball-bouncing rhymes that they know. (This activity is probably best done outside.)

3. If more than one of the students has a suggestion, pick a first student, using a counting-out rhyme from pages 31-37 of *Miss Mary Mack*.

4. Ask the students whether reciting a rhyme helps them judge the interval between bounces. What determines the amount of time a ball is in the air?

DEVELOPMENT

1. Show the students the book *Miss Mary Mack* and explain that these rhymes are common American street rhymes. Read some of the rhymes and ask whether they are familiar to the students.

2. Some of the students probably know partner clapping rhymes. Ask them to perform them for the class.

3. Have the students sit cross-legged in a circle and pass a ball or beanbag to the beat as you read some of your favorite rhymes to the class.

4. Once they're comfortable with passing one ball, add another one on the other side of the circle going in the opposite direction. Make sure the students plan their passes so the ball lands in the next person's hands directly on the beat.

RECAPITULATION

1. Divide the class into groups of four and have each group pick a rhyme to perform either with hand clapping, ball bouncing, or passing the ball.

2. Some of the rhymes have actions. See "Number One" (page 22) and "Mickey Mouse" (page 28) in *Miss Mary Mack*.

3. After giving the students time to practice, have each group perform its rhyme.

4. As the title of the book is *Miss Mary Mack*, teach the students the song by Ella Jenkins in *Holt Music*. Ask them to contribute motions.

5. For another version of the melody, play the cassette from *Shake It to the One That You Love the Best*.

CODA

1. Show the students the book *A My Name Is Alice*. Assign a letter (and verse) to each student. The boys can change the names around in the verses so they have a wife. Ask each student to work out a clapping pattern with the letter (student) next to him or her in the alphabet. The letter *Z* can pair up with the letter *A* so everyone does it twice.

2. Two other rhymes that have been put to music are "Oh, little playmate" (page 12) and "Miss Lucy had a baby" (page 14). See whether the students know the songs. They can be sung in a program with "Miss Mary Mack" and the assorted hand-clapping, ball-bouncing rhymes the students have learned.

POSSUM COME A-KNOCKIN'

By Nancy Van Laan.
Illustrated by George Booth.
New York: Alfred A. Knopf, 1990.

In this humorous rhythmic story, a possum knocks at the door of a busy extended family and is noticed only by the youngest girl, the Tom-cat, and the Coon-dawg.

Lesson grade level: 2 and up

THEME

As students perform this rhythmic story as a readers theatre with actions, an underlying chant of "knock knock knock knock" provides an ostinato figure.

RESOURCES

Caduto, Michael J., and Joseph Bruchac. "Why Possum Has a Naked Tail." In *Keepers of the Animals*, 173-175. Golden, Colo.: Fulcrum, 1991.

Vain Possum wants to impress the other Animal People at the council, so Rabbit easily tricks him into putting "special medicine" on his tail.

Crofford, Emily. *The Opossum*. Wildlife Habits & Habitat, edited by Julie Bach. New York: Crestwood House, 1990.

Complete with color photographs, this book thoroughly describes the opossum and its young and details the comatose state it can lapse into to protect itself from predators.

Scheer, George F., ed. and intro. "Why the Possum's Tail Is Bare." In *Cherokee Animal Tales*, 2nd ed., illustrated by Robert Frankenberg, 75-79. Tulsa, Okla.: Council Oak Books, 1992.

The possum is tricked into thinking his furry tail is being combed when it is actually being cut.

Steig, Jeanne. "The Opossum." In *Consider the Lemming*, pictures by William Steig. New York: Farrar, Straus & Giroux, 1988.

Combining a twist of humor with facts about opossums, this poem mentions the opossum's habit of playing dead.

KEYWORDS

Ostinato — a clearly defined phrase that is repeated consistently.

Pourquoi story — an animal folktale that explains the origin of an animal's physical characteristics. These tales are appropriately named: *Pourquoi* is French for "why."

Refrain — a recurring phrase, usually at the end of a poem or song.

EXPOSITION

1. What is a possum? Have students contribute what they know about the opossum. List their responses, adding unfamiliar terminology: for example, *prehensile* and *marsupial*.

2. Read Steig's poem "The Opossum." What does the poet think of opossums? What is *fricasseed*? Discuss the students' feelings about eating opossum.

3. Discuss the cover illustrations and title page of *Possum Come A-Knockin'*. Can the students determine the setting of the book? What is the basis for their guesses? Will the book be funny or serious? Why are the words *possum* and *a-knockin'* shortened?

Fig. 1.

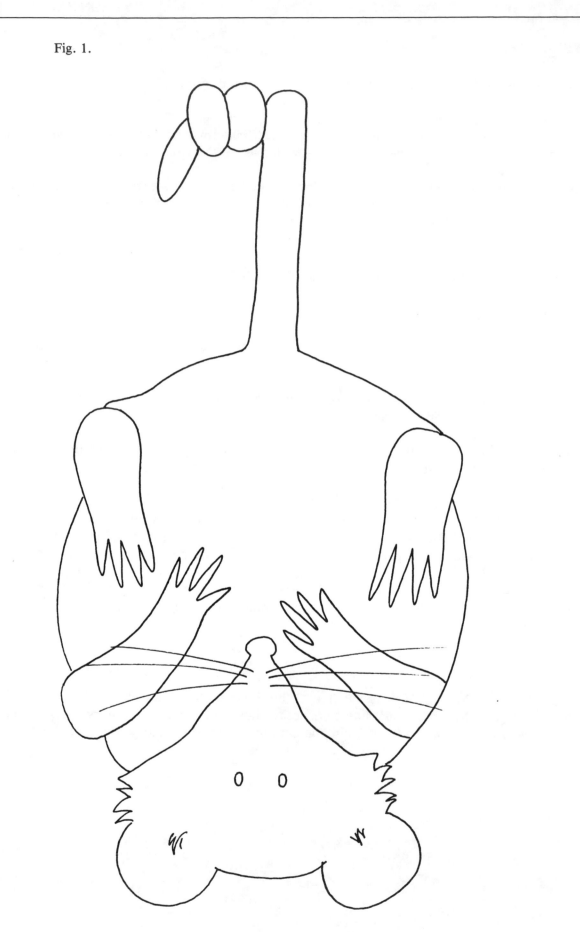

TRAIN SONG

By Diane Siebert.
Paintings by Mike Wimmer.
New York: Thomas Y. Crowell, 1990.

This rhythmic poem describes the historic trains connecting various parts of the United States.

Lesson grade level: 2 and up

THEME

Imitating the slow start and gradual acceleration of a train, students will experience the *accelerando* of music.

RESOURCES

Crews, Donald. *Freight Train*. Bedford Hills, N.Y.: Educational Enrichment Materials, 1980. 1 filmstrip, 1 sound cassette.

This filmstrip version of Crews's book is accompanied by actual train sounds and guitar music that accelerates.

"John Henry." In *Fireside Book of Folk Songs*, selected and edited by Margaret Bradford Boni, arranged for the piano by Norman Lloyd, illustrated by Alice Provensen and Martin Provensen, 170-171. New York: Simon and Schuster, 1947.

This song relates one of the legends about John Henry, a steel driver from West Virginia who with his hammer beat a steam drill in a contest.

Livingston, Myra Cohn. *Poem-Making: Ways to Begin Writing Poetry*, 78. New York: HarperCollins, 1991.

Livingston cites Stevenson's use of *trochaic* and *dactylic* feet in "From a Railway Carriage" as a method of simulating urgency and speed.

McCord, David. "Song of the Train." In *Far and Few: Rhymes of the Never Was and Always Is*, 87-88. Boston: Little, Brown, 1952.

This two-stanza poem imitates the sound of the train on the track.

Newton, Eddie. "Casey Jones." In *Fireside Book of Folk Songs*, 142-144.

The song tells the story of the famed engineer of the *Cannonball* who died at the throttle.

"O, The Train's off the Track." In *Angel at the Door: Southern Folksongs*, (compiled by) Shirley W. McRae, 11-12. St. Louis, Mo.: Magnamusic-Baton, 1981.

This Virginia folk song utilizes only four notes. An accompaniment with rhythm instruments and xylophones is included.

Siebert, Diane. "Train Song." In *The Random House Book of Poetry for Children*, selected and introduced by Jack Prelutsky, illustrated by Arnold Lobel, 222. New York: Random House, 1983.

Stevenson, Robert Louis. "From a Railway Carriage." In *The Random House Book of Poetry for Children*, 224.

Stevenson describes the view from the window of a fast-moving train.

"Train's off the Track." In *A Folk Gathering: 15 Play-Along Songs*, arranged for the elementary pianist with lots of helpers by Lynn Freeman Olson, 16-17. New York: Carl Fischer, 1982.

The American folk song is arranged for three pianists, tambourine, and sand blocks.

"The Wabash Cannonball." In *Songs of the Wild West*, (compiled by) the Metropolitan Museum of Art in association with the Buffalo Bill Historical Center, commentary by Alan Axelrod, arrangements by Dan Fox, 116-117. New York: Simon & Schuster, 1991.

The piano introduction to this railroad song imitates the sounds of the whistle and the train on the track. The piece starts slowly and gradually picks up speed.

KEYWORDS

Accelerando—a gradual quickening of the tempo.

Dactyl—a foot in poetic meter consisting of three syllables, the first accented and the following two unaccented.

Eighth note—in 4/4 meter a note with a duration of a half beat.

Half note—in 4/4 meter a note with a duration of two beats.

Quarter note—in 4/4 meter a note with a duration of one beat.

Trochee—a foot in poetic meter consisting of two syllables, the first accented and the second unaccented.

EXPOSITION

1. Begin by reading McCord's poem about a train and talk about the rhythmic motion and sounds of a train.

2. Ask how many students have ever gone on a train ride. What do they remember about the sounds and sights?

3. Ask them to give you examples of these sounds and sights. Probably some will come up with "chugga chugga choo choo." Have them clap the rhythm, and as they chant it, gradually increase the tempo.

4. Explain that Siebert's book is actually a poem that has been expanded and illustrated. Show them the poem in *The Random House Book of Poetry for Children*.

DEVELOPMENT

1. Read *Train Song* without stopping, so the students hear the rhythmic aspects. Repeat the reading and discuss the illustrations and the factual information given about trains.

2. Emphasize the rhythmic aspects of the poem and how the words imitate the sounds of the track.

3. Read the first page of the book, clapping on the syllables. Repeat them, asking the students to clap and recite them with you.

4. Write out the page beginning with "boxcars..." on chart paper. Divide the class into two groups and have them say alternate lines.

5. Explain the term *accelerando*. Conduct the students so that the poem begins slowly and gradually becomes faster. Practice until the students are comfortable with the words and rhythm.

6. Show the filmstrip *Freight Train* by Donald Crews for a visual representation of accelerando. Ask the students to listen to the guitar accompaniment to see how it corresponds to the text.

RECAPITULATION

1. Teach the students the following counting-out rhyme:

    Engine, engine number nine

    Running on Chicago line.

    If the train should jump the track,

    Do you want your money back?

2. Have them clap for each syllable, noting that the last word of each line has a longer duration.

3. Repeat the rhyme, accelerating so that the students clap only on the strong beats (four per line).

4. Finally, accelerate so that the students only clap twice per line. (The students began clapping eighth notes, then quarter notes, and, finally, half notes.)

5. Show the notation chart below and explain that as a poem or music piece becomes faster, the accents become farther apart so the poem or piece can flow. Have them try to clap the eighth notes at the accelerated speed and notice the frenzy.

6. As a class, plan a program that includes the train poems and songs listed above. Assign the poems to groups of students and practice the songs as a whole group. ("Engine, engine..." is a good introductory poem to recite before the song, "Oh, The Train's off the Track.")

CODA

1. Discuss the viewpoint these poems and songs are told from. Some are told from the vantage point of riding on the train, some from watching a train go by.

2. After brainstorming images from both viewpoints, write a pair of class poems.

3. Talk about some of the railroad legends in tall tales such as "John Henry" and "Casey Jones." Show the students some of the books on these men. Point out that these titles can be found in the folktale section of the library. Teach the songs.

Melody

All the Pretty Horses by Susan Jeffers

Fiddle-I-Fee: A Farmyard Song for the Very Young, adapted and illustrated by Melissa Sweet

Georgia Music by Helen V. Griffith

Grandma's Band by Brad Bowles

Mary Wore Her Red Dress, and Henry Wore His Green Sneakers, adapted and illustrated by Merle Peek

Sing, Pierrot, Sing: A Picture Book in Mime by Tomie dePaola

Ten Bears in My Bed: A Goodnight Countdown by Stan Mack

There's a Hole in the Bucket, pictures by Nadine Bernard Westcott

ALL THE PRETTY HORSES

By Susan Jeffers.
New York: Macmillan, 1974.

In this lullaby of the American South illustrated by the author, bedtime fears are soothed by thoughts of horses: "blacks and bays, dapples and grays."

Lesson grade level: 2 and up

THEME

The students will learn lullabies in both major keys and minor keys and discuss the differences.

RESOURCES

"All the Pretty Little Horses." In *The Fireside Book of Children's Songs*, collected and edited by Marie Winn, musical arrangements by Allan Miller, illustrations by John Alcorn, 22. New York: Simon & Schuster, 1966.

"All the Pretty Little Horses." In *Singing Bee! A Collection of Favorite Children's Songs*, compiled by Jane Hart, pictures by Anita Lobel, 11. New York: Lothrop, Lee & Shepard Books, 1982.

"Bye'm Bye." In *The Fireside Book of Children's Songs*, 13.

This lullaby numbers the stars and features an ascending melody stepping from C to G and a descending octave jump from C to C.

Dragonwagon, Crescent. *Half a Moon and One Whole Star*. Illustrations by Jerry Pinkney. New York: Macmillan, 1986.

This poem with lullaby rhythms describes the sounds and happenings of night, including crickets whirring and a musician playing his saxophone.

Larrick, Nancy, comp. *When the Dark Comes Dancing: A Bedtime Poetry Book*. Illustrated by John Wallner. New York: Philomel Books, 1983.

This collection includes lullaby lyrics and poems about night, the moon, stars, and dreams.

Yolen, Jane, ed. *The Lullaby Songbook*. With musical arrangement by Adam Stemple. Pictures by Charles Mikolaycak. San Diego, Calif.: Harcourt Brace Jovanovich, 1986.

This collection of fifteen lullabies from various cultures includes brief background notes and musical accompaniment.

KEYWORDS

Fifth—the interval made up of the first and fifth tones of a scale.

Lull—to cause to rest peacefully.

Major scale—a series of eight adjacent notes that follows this pattern of whole (W) and half (H) steps: WWHWWWH.

Minor scale—a series of eight adjacent notes that follows this pattern of whole (W) and half (H) steps: WHWWHWW.

Octave—eight tones of a scale or the interval of the first and last tones of a scale.

Scale—a series of tones within the span of an octave.

EXPOSITION

1. Ask the students whether they know the song "Rock-a-bye Baby." Sing it with them and discuss whether this would help someone fall asleep.

2. Have the students list and sing, if possible, the lullabies that their parents have sung to them. What characteristics should a lullaby have? Tell them the definition of *lull*.

3. Discuss with the students what they think about at night in order to fall asleep.

DEVELOPMENT

1. Read *All the Pretty Horses*. Discuss the illustrations. Are they soothing or lulling?

2. Sing the lullaby or play it on a xylophone. (If you play it in the key of D minor, you only need to substitute a B-flat bar on the xylophone.) Ask for the students' comments. Does the music sound sad? Does it sound better fast or slow?

3. Sing or play a descending minor scale and compare it to the phrase "go to sleepy little baby" in the lullaby.

4. Ask the students whether they notice a difference in the music in the "blacks and bays" section. Explain that this portion is in a major key, which has a sprightlier feeling.

5. Sing "Bye'm Bye," which is in a major key. Ask the students to compare its mood with that of "All the Pretty Horses."

RECAPITULATION

1. Teach "All the Pretty Little Horses" to the students. Emphasize that the first two lines have the same melody and that the descending minor scale is repeated also.

2. Teach "Bye'm Bye." Have the students hold up the number of fingers to match the stars as they're counting. Use the song as an introduction to a reading of Dragonwagon's *Half a Moon and One Whole Star*.

3. Sing and play some of the other lullabies in *The Lullaby Songbook*. Compare the scales. See whether the students can determine whether the song is in a major key or a minor key.

4. After examining the lyrics of the songs, have the students choose a lullaby to illustrate.

CODA

1. As a class, put together a list of picture books that have a bedtime or nighttime theme.

2. Plan an evening for parents in which the students read the stories, sing the lullabies, and display their illustrated lullabies. (Pajamas are optional.)

FIDDLE-I-FEE: A FARMYARD SONG FOR THE VERY YOUNG

Adapted and illustrated by Melissa Sweet.
Boston: Little, Brown, 1992.

This illustrated folk song describes a boy feeding various farmyard animals, each responding with a rhythmic sound.

Lesson grade level: Pre-K to 2

THEME

The students will investigate three melodic patterns in singing the song "Fiddle-I-Fee."

RESOURCES

Brown, Craig. *My Barn*. New York: Greenwillow Books, 1991.

As a farmer walks around his barn in the morning, he is pleased with each sound that the animals make.

"Old MacDonald Had a Farm." In *Singing Bee! A Collection of Favorite Children's Songs*, compiled by Jane Hart, pictures by Anita Lobel, 118-119. New York: Lothrop, Lee & Shepard Books, 1982.

Zimmermann, H. Werner. *Henny Penny*. New York: Scholastic, 1989.

As in *Fiddle-I-Fee*, farmyard animals join in the parade as Henny Penny travels to tell the king that the sky has fallen.

DISCOGRAPHY

Copland, Aaron. "I Bought Me a Cat." *Old American Songs: For Voice and Piano (or Orchestra)*. Mormon Tabernacle Choir, Utah Symphony Orchestra, Michael Tilson Thomas. CBS Records. MT-42140. Sound cassette.

KEYWORDS

Do (doh) — in the system of solmization (naming notes of the scale), the first scale note.

Mi (mi) — in the system of solmization, the third scale note.

Re (ray) — in the system of solmization, the second scale note.

Sol (soh) — in the system of solmization, the fifth scale note.

Solmization — a system of naming the notes of a scale by syllables instead of letters; in a major scale, the syllables are do-re-mi-fa-sol-la-ti-do.

EXPOSITION

1. Ask the students to list farmyard animals. Ask what kinds of sounds they make.

2. Read Brown's *My Barn* and show the students the printed animal sounds. Encourage them to mimic the sounds.

3. Play the Copland recording "I Bought Me a Cat." Talk about the sounds for the animals in this folk song.

4. Read *Fiddle-I-Fee*, asking the students to guess the next animal that will be fed. They will quickly notice that the next animal is previewed on the preceding page. For beginning readers, point out the highlighted animal words.

5. Show the students the song at the end of the book and sing it as you show the pictures again.

DEVELOPMENT

1. Ask the students to recall the order of the animals. Write these on a chart.

2. Next, ask for the corresponding sounds for each animal and add these to the chart. Make the chart in three columns so the students see that there are three rhythmic patterns.

Cat: fiddle-i-fee		
Hen:	chipsy, chopsy	
Duck:		quack, quack
Goose:	swishy, swashy	
Dog:	bow-wow, bow-wow	
Sheep:		baa, baa
Pig:	griffy, gruffy	
Goat:		bleat, bleat
Cow:		moo, moo

RECAPITULATION

1. Using the chart, sing the song again. Have the students join in on the animal sounds. (I learned the "fiddle-i-fee" with the syllables mi-mi-re-do.)

2. Talk about the melodic lines. Which ones step down? Which ones skip up? Which is the highest? If the students are familiar with the solmization syllables, relate them to the pitches: "fiddle-i-fee" (mi-mi-re-do), "chipsy, chopsy" (mi-sol, mi-sol), "quack, quack" (sol, sol).

3. Using the chart, point out that the sounds with the same rhythm also have the same melody.

4. Divide the class into three groups according to the three melodic lines of the animal sounds. Sing the song as a class, with the groups singing just their parts.

5. Sing "Old MacDonald Had a Farm" and point out the similarity between "E-I-E-I-O" (mi-mi-re-re-do) and "fiddle-i-fee."

CODA

1. Teach the rhythmic notation at another lesson.

2. Expand the sounds further by asking the students to assign a rhythm instrument to each animal sound in *Fiddle-I-Fee.*

3. *Henny Penny* is another story that adds farmyard animals as the story progresses. Read this story to the class and have the students choose a rhythm instrument to match each animal. Whenever the animal's name is said, a student plays the instrument.

GEORGIA MUSIC

By Helen V. Griffith.
Pictures by James Stevenson.
New York: Mulberry Books, 1990.

A young girl helps her grandfather regain his enthusiasm for life by learning to play the harmonica and re-creating the sounds of his Georgia farm.

Lesson grade level: 2 and up

THEME

Students will listen to birdcalls and bird songs, determine the melodic features, and try to mimic them with their voices or on a harmonica.

RESOURCES

Fleischman, Paul. "The Actor." In *I Am Phoenix*, illustrated by Ken Nutt, 11-12. New York: Harper & Row, 1985.

In this two-voice poem, the mockingbird describes the various ways it imitates the sounds of other birds.

Griffith, Helen V. *Grandaddy's Place*. Pictures by James Stevenson. New York: Greenwillow Books, 1987.

Janetta's first visit to Grandaddy's farm is scary, but after humorous incidents, she and her grandaddy begin to think and act alike.

Hawthorne, Alice. "Listen to the Mockingbird." In *An Illustrated Treasury of Songs*, (compiled by) the National Gallery of Art, 48. Milwaukee, Wis.: Hal Leonard; New York: Rizzoli, 1991.

Hurd, Edith Thacher. *I Dance in My Red Pajamas*. Pictures by Emily Arnold McCully. New York: Harper & Row, 1982.

Emily's parents warn her not to be noisy when she spends the night at her grandparents' house, but Emily knows she will dance in her red pajamas as her grandma plays the piano.

"Hush, Little Baby." In *Singing Bee! A Collection of Favorite Children's Songs*, compiled by Jane Hart, pictures by Anita Lobel, 12. New York: Lothrop, Lee & Shepard Books, 1982.

In this southern lullaby, "Mama's going to buy you a mockingbird."

Johnston, Tony. *Grandpa's Song*. Pictures by Brad Sneed. New York: Dial Books for Young Readers, 1991.

All of Grandpa's songs are so loud that the pictures on the wall shake when he sings. When his mind becomes fuzzy and he starts to forget even the song he made up, his grandchildren help him remember.

Robbins, Chandler S., Bertel Bruun, and Herbert S. Zim. *Birds of North America*, 168, 226-227. New York: Golden Press, 1966.

This comprehensive bird book usually describes the bird's call or song. These pages give information about the chuck-will's-widow and the mockingbird.

Steig, Jeanne. "The Mockingbird." In *Consider the Lemming*, pictures by William Steig. New York: Farrar, Straus & Giroux, 1988.

This poem extols the imitative powers of the mockingbird and calls him a "one-bird cabaret."

Whitman, Ann H., ed. *Familiar Birds of North America: Western Region*. The Audubon Society Pocket Guides. New York: Alfred A. Knopf, 1986.

Each bird is described with a color photograph and identified by appearance, voice, habitat, and range. The voice identification is especially descriptive.

KEYWORDS

Chuck-will's-widow—a bird common in pine woods of the southeastern United States that is similar to a whippoorwill and named after its call.

Harmonica—an instrument consisting of a flat, metal box containing pairs of reeds that produce adjacent notes determined by whether the player inhales or exhales; also called a *mouth organ*.

Mockingbird—a bird of the southern United States that can imitate the songs of other birds.

EXPOSITION

1. Show the students the picture on the cover of *Georgia Music*. Ask them to guess who the characters are and where the story takes place. Of course, the title will give a hint.

2. Ask whether any of their grandparents live on farms or in the South.

3. If you have already read Griffith's *Grandaddy's Place*, refer to the situations in that book.

4. Discuss how living in the country is different than living in the city. What kinds of sounds do you hear in the country that you usually do not hear in the city?

DEVELOPMENT

1. Read *Georgia Music*, stopping to discuss the birds and insects mentioned in the story.

2. Read "The Actor" with another person. Discuss the verbs Fleischman uses to describe the mockingbird's imitations of other birds' sounds.

3. If possible play a tape of the songs of mockingbirds and chuck-will's-widows. Ask the students to describe each bird's song. Is it high, low, ascending, descending, skipping, or stepping? Define the word *mocking* and explain how birds are often named after their calls.

4. Explain how a harmonica works and demonstrate the scale tones and the chords. Would the girl in the story be able to imitate the sounds she heard in the country?

RECAPITULATION

1. Ask students to try to capture sounds of birds on tape by setting up a tape recorder in their backyards. Discuss the best times of the day to hear these sounds. If you can, assign this over the weekend so that it will be possible for city-dwelling students to go into the country.

2. Play the tapes and see whether anyone can identify the bird. Have the students describe the pitches and/or melodic lines.

3. Set up a birdcall identification center so students can become familiar with common birdcalls and bird songs.

4. If any of your students own harmonicas, ask them to try to imitate a bird sound for the class to identify.

CODA

1. Teach the students "Listen to the Mockingbird" and "Hush, Little Baby."

2. Read *Grandpa's Song* as another example of children who help their grandpa to remember.

3. Read *I Dance in My Red Pajamas* as another example of children and grandparents interacting through music.

4. Have the students listen to bird-song tapes and match the tones. Ask them to describe whether the melody is ascending or descending and in skips or steps.

5. Read Steig's "The Mockingbird." Discuss all the musical terms, such as *cacophony* and *repertoire*.

GRANDMA'S BAND

By Brad Bowles.
Designed and illustrated by Anthony Chan.
Owings Mills, Md.: Stemmer House, 1989.

Bored with washing clothes, Grandma discovers a musical use for her washboard. As she sings old songs, she is joined one by one by the farmyard animals, a fox, and a wolf.

Lesson grade level: Pre-K to 2

THEME

This participatory book of story and song teaches some traditional American songs and allows students to echo the melodies with animal sounds.

RESOURCES

"The Animal Fair." In *The Fireside Book of Children's Songs*, collected and edited by Marie Winn, musical arrangements by Allan Miller, illustrations by John Alcorn, 152-153. New York: Simon & Schuster, 1966.

These words are slightly different than the ones in *Grandma's Band*.

"Crawdad Song." In *An Illustrated Treasury of Songs*, (compiled by) the National Gallery of Art, 90. Milwaukee, Wis.: Hal Leonard; New York: Rizzoli, 1991.

Beginning with "You get a line and I'll get a pole," this traditional folk song has five other verses.

Livingston, Myra Cohn, comp. *Poems for Grandmothers*. Illustrated by Patricia Cullen-Clark. New York: Holiday House, 1990.

This collection of eighteen poems celebrates all types of grandmothers.

"On Top of Old Smoky." In *An Illustrated Treasury of Songs*, 7.

This Appalachian folk song has four verses.

"She'll Be Comin' 'Round the Mountain." In *An Illustrated Treasury of Songs*, 56-57.

This railroad song includes six verses but does not include the exclamations I learned, such as "whoa boy" and "hack hack."

EXPOSITION

1. Ask the students how many of them have a grandma who sings. Does she sing old songs? Does she sing to them?

2. Have the students describe their grandmas. Ask whether any of these grandmothers live on farms.

3. Have assembled the musical implements you will need: a washboard, thimble, metal cup, and assorted jars and pans. (A granny outfit can be effective, but because grandmas come in all styles these days, it isn't essential.)

4. Show the students the title page and half-title page and tell them the title of Bowles's book. Can the students guess the type of band Grandma will have and where she lives?

DEVELOPMENT

1. Read the first page of *Grandma's Band* and have the students predict what is going to happen. On the second page let them name all the things she could be doing other than washing clothes.

2. As you read the part about scraping the thimble across the washboard, join in with your thimble and washboard.

3. Teach the chant on page 10 of *Grandma's Band* so the students can chant along with your washboard beat.

4. When you get to the page where she is banging on all kinds of pots, pans, and jars, let a few students join you with drumsticks. They can accompany you as you sing "You get a line...." Sing the song a couple of times so the students learn the melody and lyrics.

5. As the animals start to appear and join in the singing, sing their parts as an echo to your last melodic line. After you sing it, have the students sing it.

RECAPITULATION

1. After you finish the book, teach the students the songs they didn't know. The "Crawdad Song" and "The Animal Fair" may be unfamiliar.

2. Review the sounds the animals make and practice them until all of the students can do them alone. Practice by having students match your melody with the animal sound.

3. Assign animal parts to groups of students so that everyone in the class can participate. You already have a couple of students assigned to playing the pots, pans, and jars. Probably you should remain Grandma.

4. In order to cue the animal parts, provide pictures of the animals on sticks or on the board, so you can point to them when it's that animal's turn to sing.

5. Read the book again with everyone participating.

CODA

1. Combine this book with other picture books and poems for a Grandmother Day.

2. Read *Grandpa's Song* by Tony Johnston (see page 25) for some old favorites sung by a grandpa.

MARY WORE HER RED DRESS,
AND HENRY WORE HIS GREEN SNEAKERS

Adapted and illustrated by Merle Peek.
New York: Clarion Books, 1985.

In this dramatized folk song, a new color is added to the illustrations as a new person wearing a different color arrives at Katy's birthday party.

Lesson grade level: Pre-K to 2

THEME
Using songs about clothing and colors, students will learn the pentatonic scale common in many folk songs.

RESOURCES
"Jennie Jenkins." In *The Best Singing Games for Children of All Ages*, (compiled by) Edgar S. Bley, 40-41. New York: Sterling, 1976.

Jennie refuses to wear seven different colors until, in the eighth verse, she decides to go bare.

"Jennie Jenkins." In *Go In and Out the Window: An Illustrated Songbook for Young People*, music arranged and edited by Dan Fox, commentary by Claude Marks, 76-77. New York: Metropolitan Museum of Art, 1987.

Jennie is asked whether she'll wear blue, green, and so on, but none of the colors will do.

"Mary Wore a Red Dress." In *Jim Along, Josie: A Collection of Folk Songs and Singing Games for Young Children*, compiled by Nancy Langstaff and John Langstaff, illustrated by Jan Pienkowski, 60. New York: Harcourt Brace Jovanovich, 1970.

This version includes a part for chime bars, and ostinatos for percussion and any tuned instrument.

KEYWORDS
Glockenspiel—a tuned percussion instrument that consists of a series of flat steel bars of different lengths that are attached to a frame.

Pentatonic scale—a scale made up of five tones, the most common consisting of CDFGA.

EXPOSITION

1. Alert the students that they will have to use their skills of observation and memory with this story. Prepare them by asking for their observations about the endpaper pictures and the title page. Point out the squirrel walking on the path.

2. Read the first two pages and ask the students what changed in the illustrations. (Each character is wearing a different color, and the colors added to the illustrations are cumulative.)

3. Encourage the students to join in once they recognize the pattern. Have them guess who wore the pink hat. They must remember who wore the yellow sweater.

DEVELOPMENT

1. Show the students the music at the end of the book. Play the tune on the glockenspiel, singing the verses for "Mary wore her red dress" and "Henry wore his green sneakers."

2. Go through the book again, singing the song with the students.

3. Begin singing the song, incorporating the names of children in the class and the clothing they're wearing. Ask the students to join in on "All day long."

4. Sing about each person in the class. Ask the students to suggest clothing that classmates are wearing. Put these suggestions into new verses, for instance: Amy wore her polka-dot dress.

5. You can also use this as an exercise in matching pitches by asking the question "Who wore her pink sweater?" and having that student answer on the same pitches, "I wore my pink sweater." The whole class can join in on "All day long."

6. Remove the E and B glockenspiel bars and discuss the pentatonic scale. If there is a keyboard available, point out that the black keys are a pentatonic scale.

RECAPITULATION

1. If you have a number of glockenspiels or xylophones, teach small groups to play parts of the song. For younger children, "All day long" is sufficient.

2. Divide the class into three groups: one for singing, one for acting, and one for playing.

3. List the students' suggestions for names and apparel on chart paper so the students can read them as they sing. If you are doing this with students who cannot read, draw a picture of the clothing.

4. Have the students who are wearing the clothing cross the area, performing any kind of action they wish. Discuss possible actions before you begin.

5. Perform the song three times so that each group can sing, act, and play.

CODA

1. Teach the children the song "Jennie Jenkins," using the suggestions in *The Best Singing Games for Children of All Ages*.

2. *Go In and Out the Window* has chorus words that are more fun to sing.

3. Have the students make up their own rhyming words for other color verses.

SING, PIERROT, SING: A PICTURE BOOK IN MIME

by Tomie dePaola.
London: Methuen, 1983.

This wordless picture book depicts the classic mime character Pierrot in his futile attempt to court his love.

Lesson grade level: 2 and up

THEME

"Au Clair de la Lune" is played as an introduction to the classic story of the mime Pierrot's quest for love. In learning the folk song, students will recognize repeated melodic lines and a descending five-note pattern.

RESOURCES

"Au Clair de la Lune." In *Fireside Book of Folk Songs*, selected and edited by Margaret Bradford Boni, arranged for the piano by Norman Lloyd, illustrated by Alice Provensen and Martin Provensen, 74-75. New York: Simon & Schuster, 1947.

This version has four verses and attributes the melody to Jean Baptiste Lully, a seventeenth-century French composer in the court of Louis XIV.

"Au Clair de la Lune." In *The Golden Song Book*, selected and arranged by Katharine Tyler Wessells, illustrated by Kathy Allert, 43. New York: Golden Press, 1981.

The first verse is given in French and English.

"Au Clair de la Lune." In *The Usborne Children's Songbook*, compiled by Heather Amery, illustrated by Stephen Cartwright, music arrangements by Barrie Carson Turner, 46-47. London: Usborne, 1988.

This version has three verses in French.

Benet's Reader's Encyclopedia, 3rd ed., 202, 426, 763. New York: Harper & Row, 1987.

The stock characters Columbine (or Pierrette), Harlequin, and Pierrot are defined as they appeared in Italian commedia dell'arte.

"The Mulberry Bush." In *Singing Bee! A Collection of Favorite Children's Songs*, compiled by Jane Hart, pictures by Anita Lobel, 80. New York: Lothrop, Lee & Shepard Books, 1982.

KEYWORDS

Mime — an actor who plays a part with mimic gesture and action, usually without words.

Pantomime or mime — a silent drama using gesture, facial expression, and movement, based on sixteenth-century Italian commedia dell'arte.

Pierrot — a romantic clown character of old Italian drama and pantomime whose face is covered with white flour or powder and who wears a white, voluminous garment with big sleeves.

EXPOSITION

1. As the students settle around you, do not speak. Show with gestures that you want complete silence. Once everyone is attentive, play the tune "Au Clair de la Lune" on a stringed instrument, keyboard, or flute.

2. Still without speaking, show the picture book to the students, mimicking Pierrot's gestures as appropriate.

DEVELOPMENT

1. Tell the students the title of the book and explain that Pierrot is the name of the main character.

2. Ask the students to recount the story line as you again show the pictures in the book.

3. Discuss the term *pantomime* and talk about how a mime tells a story or acts a part. Explain that Pierrot likes Pierrette but that the Harlequin is Pierrot's rival for her love.

4. Point out that Pierrot's white face is like a mask hiding his feelings.

5. Discuss the costumes and relate that Pierrot always wore the white garment and the Harlequin always wore the parti-colored costume. In this way, the audience always knew the characters in the pantomime.

RECAPITULATION

1. Play the song again and ask the students to tell you whether any of the melody lines are the same.

2. Because three of the four lines are the same melody, teach this first, using the syllable *loo*.

3. Teach the third line, which has a different melody, pointing out the descending five tones.

4. If ambitious, teach the French words.

5. Give each student a precut, white posterboard face and black, blue, and red markers. Ask them to draw Pierrot's features using dePaola's illustrations as a guide.

6. Attach the masks to dowels or to the cardboard tubing from hangers.

CODA

1. Have students pantomime various tasks using the song "The Mulberry Bush," which includes "This is the way we brush our teeth," and so on.

2. When they are comfortable with these dramatics, assign groups to pantomime a story.

TEN BEARS IN MY BED: A GOODNIGHT COUNTDOWN

By Stan Mack.
New York: Pantheon Books, 1974.

In this countdown-to-bedtime book, a boy asks the ten bears in his bed to roll over, and each leaves the room on one of the boy's toys.

Lesson grade level: Pre-K to 2

THEME

Students master a descending broken triad, sol-mi-do, as they sing the song "Roll Over."

RESOURCES

Ahlberg, Allan. "Too Many Bears." In *Ten in a Bed*, illustrated by Andre Amstutz, 7-16. New York: Viking Kestrel, 1989.

One night a little girl discovers the Three Bears from the Goldilocks story in her bed, and they won't leave until she tells them a story.

Brett, Jan, reteller. *Goldilocks and the Three Bears*. New York: G. P. Putnam's Sons, 1987.

This traditional retelling is set in a Bavarian forest. Brett uses her trademark borders to fore-shadow events in the story.

Peek, Merle. *Roll Over: A Counting Song*. New York: Houghton Mifflin, 1981.

The illustrations in this version of the song show various animals rolling out of the bed. At the end of the story, they are in the wallpaper border.

"Roll Over." In *Singing Bee! A Collection of Favorite Children's Songs*, compiled by Jane Hart, pictures by Anita Lobel, 21. New York: Lothrop, Lee & Shepard Books, 1982.

"Ten in a Bed." In *The Usborne Children's Songbook*, compiled by Heather Amery, illustrated by Stephen Cartwright, music arrangements by Barrie Carson Turner, 10-11. London: Usborne, 1988.

Wood, Audrey. *The Napping House*, illustrated by Don Wood. San Diego, Calif.: Harcourt Brace Jovanovich, 1984.

Instead of having animals roll over and leave, this cumulative tale adds people and animals until no one is napping.

KEYWORDS

Broken triad—a chord consisting of two thirds sung melodically.

Kodaly hand signs—a system developed by Hungarian composer Zoltan Kodaly for teaching scale tones with a corresponding hand signal (see figure 2).

Solmization—a system of naming the notes of a scale by syllables instead of letters; in a major scale the syllables are do-re-mi-fa-sol-la-ti-do.

EXPOSITION

1. Read a version of *Goldilocks and the Three Bears*, with the students joining in on the familiar phrases.

2. Ask the students whether any of them have ever slept with a stuffed bear. (If this is a young group and part of a bear unit, you may have invited them to bring their bears to school.)

3. Tell the students that having bears in your bed can be a problem. Look at the title page of *Ten Bears in My Bed* and discuss the amount of room left for the boy.

Fig. 2.

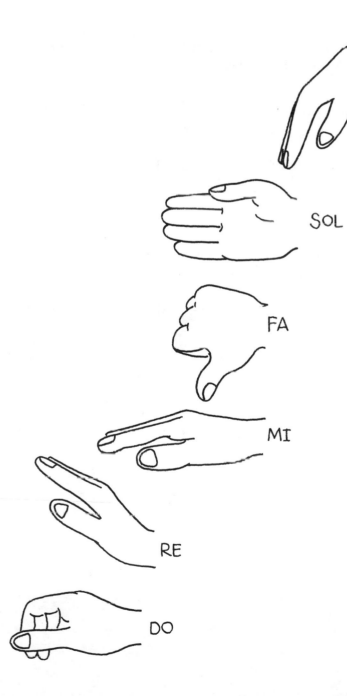

DEVELOPMENT

1. Read *Ten Bears in My Bed*. The students will probably join in and say, "one fell out." Allow them to guess what number you are on as you turn the page. Also ask them to guess the verb used to describe the bear that is leaving.

2. After reading a couple of the pages, start singing the "roll over" on a descending triad (sol-mi-do).

3. Ask the students to join you. The "good night" is simply sol-mi.

4. Discuss the illustration on the last page, in which all the toys are back and the bears are in the boy's dreams.

RECAPITULATION

1. Teach the entire song from *The Singing Bee!* or *Usborne*, adding the Kodaly hand signs for sol-mi-do and singing the syllables. Younger students enjoy using the hand signs, which reinforce the skipping downward of the melody.

2. Ask the group to think of different ways the bears could leave. Give examples, such as moon-danced out, somersaulted out, and so on. List the actions from one to ten on chart paper.

3. Choose two students to perform actions listed on the chart paper while the rest of the class sings the song. Repeat the song with ten different actors so that all ten actions are performed.

CODA

1. Read the chapter on the three bears from Ahlberg's *Ten in a Bed*. You may have to skip some parts to shorten it. Compare the story to the traditional one with Goldilocks.

2. Read *The Napping House*. Ask the students whether this is similar to *Ten Bears in My Bed*. Discuss how the animals are added instead of taken away.

THERE'S A HOLE IN THE BUCKET

Pictures By Nadine Bernard Westcott.
New York: Harper & Row, 1990.

In this illustrated version of the folk song, Henry follows Liza's advice for fixing the hole in the bucket but ends up right where he started.

Lesson grade level: 3 and up

THEME

The importance of a keynote in tonality is reinforced by comparing the return to the keynote in "There's a Hole in the Bucket" to the return to Liza after each of Henry's attempts to fix the hole in the bucket.

RESOURCES

"Draw a Bucket of Water." In *Jim Along, Josie: A Collection of Folk Songs and Singing Games for Young Children*, compiled by Nancy Langstaff and John Langstaff, illustrated by Jan Pienkowski, 78. New York: Harcourt Brace Jovanovich, 1970.

This version is similar in melody and actions to "Sugar Bowl"; however, it does not include the hopping.

Hart, Jane, comp. *Singing Bee! A Collection of Favorite Children's Songs*. Pictures by Anita Lobel. New York: Lothrop, Lee & Shepard Books, 1982.

Contains "Old MacDonald Had a Farm" (pages 118-119) and "Roll Over" (page 121), both of which have well-defined tonality.

Numeroff, Laura Joffe. *If You Give a Moose a Muffin*. Illustrated by Felicia Bond. New York: HarperCollins, 1991.

If you give a moose a muffin, one thing leads to another until you are back at the beginning, giving him another muffin.

"Sugar Bowl." In *Punchinella 47: Twenty Traditional American Play Parties for Singing, Dancing, and Playing Orff Instruments*, (compiled and arranged by) Tossi Aaron, 20-21. Philadelphia, Pa.: Coda, 1983.

Using singing and chanting, sets of four students imitate drawing water from a well and hop in a circle as all four form a sugar bowl.

KEYWORDS

Clef—a sign at the beginning of a staff that locates the pitch of one of the notes in the staff, thus designating the position of all the other pitches.

Keynote—the tonic, or first, note of a scale, forming the basis of the melody and harmony of a piece; sometimes referred to as the *home tone*.

Tonality—a principle of music that relates all tones of a piece to a central tone, or keynote.

Treble clef—the clef sign that locates the G above middle C on the staff.

EXPOSITION

1. Read a story to the students that is circular or ends where it began. For instance, *If You Give a Moose a Muffin* begins with giving a moose a muffin, which leads to many other incidents and finally ends with giving a moose another muffin.

2. Discuss what the author must do to achieve a story that goes in a circle or keeps coming back to the same place. Does each step have to be logical?

3. Read *There's a Hole in the Bucket*, discussing on each page the path Henry takes. Point out that he always comes back to Liza for more instructions.

4. On a piece of chart paper put Liza's name in the middle and draw the various paths Henry took to perform the tasks she suggested. Draw or label the articles at the ends of the paths.

DEVELOPMENT

1. Sing the song and ask the students to listen for recurring patterns in the melody.

2. Discuss the notes for the phrases "the bucket," "dear Liza," and "dear Henry." Show the students the music at the back of the book.

3. Point out that the treble clef is also the G clef and that the symbol encircles the line for the G note. Thus, the G is the easiest note to find on the treble staff.

4. Ask the students to count the number of G's in the treble clef melody. Explain that this is the keynote and that tonal music continually returns to its keynote and ends on its keynote.

5. Point out the chord symbols above the staff and the predominance of the G chord.

6. Teach the song by rote or notes, depending on the sophistication of the group. Point out that the half note, or longest note, B, appears on the important words in the song.

RECAPITULATION

1. After the students have had time to practice the song, divide them into two groups, with the boys singing Henry's verses and the girls singing Liza's.

2. Add the chords for harmony with keyboard, guitar, or autoharp.

3. Show the students other songs and see whether they can determine the tonality by the ending note and the predominant chords. ("Old MacDonald Had a Farm" and "Roll Over" are good examples from *Singing Bee*.)

4. "Draw a Bucket of Water" relates to *There's a Hole in the Bucket*, both in subject matter and tonality. Both it and "Sugar Bowl" are fun to learn because of the actions.

CODA

1. To continue the theme of returning to a "home tone," have the students think of folktales that have a recurring action, usually in threes. For instance, in "The Three Little Pigs," the big bad wolf huffs and puffs at three different houses. Rumpelstiltskin returns three times to allow the maiden to guess his name.

Form & Style

Bonjour, Mr. Satie by Tomie dePaola

The Complete Story of the Three Blind Mice by John W. Ivimey

Joyful Noise: Poems for Two Voices by Paul Fleischman

Mama Don't Allow by Thacher Hurd

Nathaniel Talking by Eloise Greenfield

Rondo in C by Paul Fleischman

BONJOUR, MR. SATIE

By Tomie dePaola.
New York: G. P. Putnam's Sons, 1991.

During his visit to Centerville, U.S.A., Mr. Satie, world-traveling cat, relates to his niece and nephew his experience in Paris judging an art contest between Picasso and Matisse. Well known artists, musicians, and writers are portrayed at Gertrude Stein's salon.

Lesson grade level: 4 and up

THEME

Students discover how difficult it is to compare works of art, whether visual or musical, as they learn about the paintings of Matisse and Picasso and the musical works of Gershwin and Satie.

RESOURCES

Hurd, Michael. "Satie." In *Oxford Junior Companion to Music*, 2nd ed., 289. London: Oxford University Press, 1979.

_____. "Thomson." In *Oxford Junior Companion to Music*, 326.

Mitchell, Barbara. *America, I Hear You: A Story About George Gershwin*. Illustrations by Jan Hosking Smith. Minneapolis, Minn.: Carolrhoda Books, 1987.

This fictionalized account of Gershwin's life presents facts and musical works in an easy-to-read format.

Raboff, Ernest. *Henri Matisse*. Art for Children. New York: J. B. Lippincott, 1988.

Raboff includes fifteen color reproductions of Matisse's paintings and discusses his use of color and his favorite subjects.

Satie, Erik. "Gymnopedie No. 1." In *Easy Piano Classics*, (compiled by) Philip Hawthorn, edited by Jenny Tyler and Helen Davies, music arrangements by Daniel Scott, 59. Usborne Learn to Play. Tulsa, Okla.: EDC, 1990.

This is a simplified version of Satie's original piano piece.

Venezia, Mike. *Picasso*. Getting to Know the World's Greatest Artists. Chicago: Children's Press, 1988.

This easy-to-read description of Picasso's art includes reproductions of many of his works.

DISCOGRAPHY

Gershwin, George. "An American in Paris." *Gershwin*. The London Festival Orchestra, Stanley Black. London Treasury. 417 098-4. Sound cassette.

Satie, Erik. "Gymnopedie No. 1." *Greatest Classical Melodies*. Charles Gerhardt, National Philharmonic. RCA Victor. BMG Music, 1992. 09026-60932-4. Sound cassette.

This recording features an orchestral version of Satie's piano piece.

KEYWORDS

Baker, Josephine (1906-1975) — a ragtime dancer from St. Louis, Missouri, who became the rage of Paris and later starred in the Ziegfeld Follies.

Duncan, Isadora (1878-1927) — an American dancer who performed barefoot with flowing scarves and whose dancing style was the forerunner of America's modern dance movement.

Gershwin, George (1898-1937) — an American composer who legitimized jazz by using it in classical forms.

Matisse, Henri (1869-1954) — a French painter and sculptor who is best known for his bold colors.

Picasso, Pablo (1881-1973) — a Spanish painter who spent most of his life in France and is especially known for his Cubist works.

KEYWORDS—*Continued*

Salon—a term referring to both an elegant French apartment and a meeting place where aspiring writers, painters, and musicians would share ideas.

Satie, Erik (1866-1925)—a French composer outside the mainstream of music who poked fun at musical forms and styles both in his compositions and his music titles.

Stein, Gertrude (1874-1946)—an American author who lived mainly in Paris from 1903 until her death and was a patron of Picasso, Matisse, and numerous writers.

Thomson, Virgil (1896-1989)—an American composer influenced by Satie who wrote two operas with lyrics by Gertrude Stein.

EXPOSITION

1. Ask the students which they like the best: pizza or ice cream. Discuss whether it's difficult to choose, because they are different types of food and could both be appreciated at different times.

2. Next show the students illustrations from two picture books. The illustrations of Tomie dePaola and Steven Kellogg provide a good contrast. Use Kellogg's illustrations for *Paul Bunyan* or *Ralph's Secret Weapon* to point out the differences in the two illustrators' depictions of people. Ask the students to choose which illustrations they prefer. Some students will respond that they cannot make the choice.

3. Discuss the difficulty of choosing the "best" when it is largely determined by personal taste.

4. Before you read *Bonjour, Mr. Satie*, tell the students that although this is a picture book, it addresses the universal theme of differences in artistic style and taste.

5. Explain that Mr. Satie's name comes from the French composer Erik Satie and that the characters depicted in the Paris scenes in the book were famous artists living in Paris in the early 1900s.

DEVELOPMENT

1. Read the story. Discuss the term *salon* and show the students the list of people on the dust jacket. (If the students have read *Ragtime Tumpie*, they will recognize Josephine Baker.)

2. Ask the students to describe the art of Matisse and Picasso. What is different about their artistic styles?

3. Give the students background information on Gershwin, Satie, and Thomson.

4. Play a recording of Gershwin's "An American in Paris" and Satie's "Gymnopedie No. 1." Ask the students to describe the styles. What is the mood of each piece? Can they hum the tunes? Besides the difference in instrumentation, can they describe the texture of the sound: for instance, is it sparse or full?

5. Tell the students that Erik Satie once wrote a piece entitled "Three Pieces in the Shape of a Pear," which was his way of poking fun at musical form. Satie rebelled against the musical forms and styles of the day; many of his titles were satirical.

RECAPITULATION

1. Using various art books and art reproductions, compare the art of Picasso and Matisse. Venezia's book offers clear explanations of Picasso's various periods.

2. Assign reproductions of the paintings to groups. Ask them to describe the painting in terms of shape, color, and texture. Also, what mood does the painting convey?

3. Discuss whether the same criteria of shape, color, and texture can be applied to musical works.

4. As a group, listen to portions of the recordings again and brainstorm descriptions of their shapes, colors, and textures.

CODA

1. After doing further research into the musicians and painters in *Bonjour, Mr. Satie*, see whether the students can take on the personas of various characters. Stage a salon gathering and have the characters talk to each other about their art.

THE COMPLETE STORY OF THE THREE BLIND MICE

By John W. Ivimey.
Illustrated by Paul Galdone.
New York: Clarion Books, 1987.

Embellishing the familiar nursery rhyme, Ivimey relates how the mice became blind and how they recovered.

Lesson grade level: 2 and up

THEME
Students learn to sing "Three Blind Mice" in a round and investigate the harmony of other rounds.

RESOURCES
"Three Blind Mice." In *The Mother Goose Songbook*, (compiled by) Tom Glazer, illustrated by David McPhail, 87-88. New York: Doubleday, 1990.

"Three Myopic Rodents." In *The Fireside Book of Fun and Games Songs*, collected and edited by Marie Winn, musical arrangements by Allan Miller, illustrations by Whitney Darrow, Jr., 126-127. New York: Simon & Schuster, 1974.

This version of "Three Blind Mice" has been retouched with the help of a thesaurus.

Winn, Marie, comp. and ed. "Rounds." In *The Fireside Book of Children's Songs*, musical arrangements by Allan Miller, 185-190. New York: Simon & Schuster, 1966.

This collection of ten common rounds includes a brief description on singing rounds and provides marked entrances for each voice.

Yolen, Jane, ed. and comp. *Rounds About Rounds.* Musical arrangements by Barbara Green. Illustrations by Gail Gibbons. New York: Franklin Watts, 1977.

This collection of fifty-seven rounds includes a history of rounds and advice for teaching and singing them.

DISCOGRAPHY
Pachelbel, Johann. "Canon." *Greatest Classical Melodies.* Ettore Stratta, English Chamber Orchestra. RCA Victor. BMG Music, 1992. 09026-60932-4. Sound cassette.

KEYWORDS
Canon — a musical composition in which a melody in one part is repeated later in one or more other parts, often overlapping the original melody.

Chord — a group of three or more notes sounded at the same time.

Round — a circle, or perpetual canon, in which each singer returns from the conclusion of the melody to its beginning, repeating it indefinitely.

Triad — a chord made up of two thirds; for example, a C triad consists of the notes C-E-G.

EXPOSITION

1. Show the students the cover or spine title of *Three Blind Mice* and ask them to recite the nursery rhyme with you.

2. Because many nursery rhymes have been taught by rote, with no emphasis on the meaning, ask the students their interpretation of the story. Who cut off the tails? Why did she do it? How can blind mice run after anyone?

3. Show the students the title on the title page, which begins with the words "The complete story...." Explain that Ivimey added to the rhyme to explain how the mice became blind.

4. Give the students some background information on Ivimey and Mother Goose rhymes "Three Blind Mice" was first printed in *Ravenscroft's Deuteromelia* in 1609 (Yolen, *Rounds About Rounds*, 98).

DEVELOPMENT

1. Read *The Complete Story of the Three Blind Mice*, pointing out the repeated lines and the rhymes.

2. Teach the students the song, emphasizing the three descending notes on "three blind mice." Sing each recurrent description that is sung to these notes ("three bold mice," "three cold mice," etc.).

3. Ask the students to compare the above phrase to the phrase "see how they run." Point out that it, too, is a descending phrase of three tones, but it starts at a pitch two notes higher. Ask one half of the class to sing "three blind mice" while the other half sings "see how they run." Discuss the harmony of the thirds.

4. Have the students sing "Three Blind Mice" while you accompany on any instrument with a C triad. Point out that only one chord is used throughout the song. Show the C chord notation on the treble staff.

5. Explain the terms *canon* and *round*. Ask whether any of the students have ever sung a round.

6. Try singing "Three Blind Mice" in a round with two parts. Arrange ahead how many times the groups will sing the song.

RECAPITULATION

1. Show the students the "Rounds" section in *The Fireside Book of Children's Songs*. Point out the starting notes for each section in the rounds. Put them on a staff so the students notice that the beginning notes form a chord.

2. Teach "Frère Jacques" and try as a round.

3. Practice singing *The Complete Story of the Three Blind Mice* for a performance for a younger class. Sing the first and last verses as rounds and the others straight through.

CODA

1. Have the students make a mural showing the saga of the mice. If formatted in a circle, there is a visual reminder of the round.

2. Play a recording of Pachelbel's "Canon in D." See whether the students can hear when the melody is repeated.

JOYFUL NOISE: POEMS FOR TWO VOICES

By Paul Fleischman.
Illustrated by Eric Beddows.
New York: Harper & Row, 1988.

The carefully chosen words and scientific accuracy of these insect poems for two voices add to the joy of the well-crafted poetry.

Lesson grade level: 4 and up

THEME

Students discover the elements of good ensemble speaking by relating Fleischman's two-voice poems to musical duets.

RESOURCES

Carle, Eric. *The Very Quiet Cricket*. New York: Philomel Books, 1990.

Despite greetings from many insects, a cricket is very quiet until he meets another cricket. The microchip cricket sound that is activated at the end of the book is a delight for reader and listener alike.

Fleischman, Paul. "Newbery Medal Acceptance." *The Horn Book Magazine* 65 (July/August 1989): 442-451.

In this acceptance speech for the Newbery Medal for *Joyful Noise*, Fleischman recounts how many of his interests, most importantly music, contributed to his eventual creation of this book.

KEYWORDS

Canon—a musical composition in which a melody in one part is repeated later in one or more other parts, often overlapping the original melody.

Duet—a piece for two performers.

Emphasis—a prominence given to a syllable or word by stressing it with pitch or loudness.

Ensemble—a term used to describe members of a group playing together; also, the quality of playing as a group or unified whole.

Inflection—a term that denotes a change in the pitch or loudness of the voice.

Pace—the rate at which a speech is delivered or performed.

Requiem—a musical piece honoring the dead, based on the requiem mass, the Latin word *requiem* meaning "rest."

Serenade—a love song sung at night.

Tempo—rate of speed at which a piece of music is performed.

EXPOSITION

1. Ask the students whether they can think of similarities between music and poetry. Discuss the melodic line and rhythmic meters.

2. Show them the cover of *Joyful Noise* and discuss the term *voices*. Explain that in music, *voices* does not necessarily refer to the human voice but may be a melodic part for an instrument. Introduce the word *duet*.

3. Ask whether anyone in the group has played a duet with someone. Why is it difficult to play music with someone else? Introduce the term *ensemble*, meaning both a group of performers and the quality of blending individual parts to present a concerted sound. Discuss the importance of ensemble.

4. Read Fleischman's "Grasshoppers" with another teacher.

5. Ask the students for their comments on the ensemble. Was it synchronized?

DEVELOPMENT

1. Show the students the format of the poems in *Joyful Noise* and read the instructions in the "Note."

2. Tell the students about Fleischman's use of musical concepts such as phrasing, meters, and ensemble playing in his writing (see the *Horn Book Magazine* article).

3. Discuss the importance of pacing and rhythm in reading with another person.

4. Read the beginning of Carle's *The Very Quiet Cricket* and then let the students hear the cricket sound at the end. Have them imitate the cricket sound as a class. See whether they can all say it simultaneously.

5. Read Fleischman's "House Crickets" with another teacher, pausing to cue in the class on the word *cricket*.

6. Read Fleischman's "Whirligig Beetles" with a partner. Discuss the delay in the second part. Compare this to a canon such as "Three Blind Mice."

7. What happens if one reader goes faster? Discuss the importance of inflection and emphasis.

8. Reread "Grasshoppers" and have the students listen for these elements.

RECAPITULATION

1. Using multiple copies of the book, assign poems to partners.

2. Ask the students to note any references to music. Discuss the terms *serenade* and *requiem* before the students begin to practice. "Cicadas" includes many musical terms and also contains the reference to the title, *Joyful Noise*.

3. After sufficient practice have two groups read to each other. Supply a rating sheet with checkpoints for pace, inflection, emphasis, and performing ensemble.

4. Present the poems to a class that is studying insects. (Headbands with pipe-cleaner antennae are very effective props.)

CODA

1. Have students bring in music or tapes that have insects in the title.

2. Organize a program that includes poetry duets and musical duets.

MAMA DON'T ALLOW

By Thacher Hurd.
New York: Harper & Row, 1984.

Miles and the Swamp Band are saved from becoming the main course at the Alligator Ball when they play the "Lullaby of Swampland."

Lesson grade level: 2 and up

THEME

The origins of jazz are discussed as students learn the song "Mama Don't Allow" with its blue notes and accompany themselves using homemade instruments and scat singing.

RESOURCES

Carlin, Richard. *Jazz*. The World of Music. New York: Facts on File, 1991.

This comprehensive history of jazz from its African roots to Branford Marsalis includes bibliographies and discographies for each chapter.

Cobblestone 4, "The Jazz Sensation" (October 1983).

This entire issue is devoted to jazz and includes articles on its African roots and on New Orleans as the cradle of jazz. Directions are given for making "Cigar Box Strings" and other simple instruments.

Hentoff, Nat. *Journey into Jazz*. With drawings by David Stone Martin. New York: Coward, McCann & Geoghegan, 1968.

Peter Parker has always had "strong musical feelings." After perfecting his trumpet playing, he attempts to play with a neighborhood jazz band, only to be sent away until he finally learns to play with other people and express his own feelings.

Hoban, Russell. *Emmet Otter's Jug-Band Christmas*. Pictures by Lillian Hoban. New York: Parents' Magazine Press, 1971.

Emmet and his mother both secretly enter a talent show to win the prize money for each other, but to pay the entrance fee, they both sell an item needed for their respective livelihoods.

Hunter, Ilene, and Marilyn Judson. *Simple Folk Instruments to Make and to Play*, 34-35, 124, 128. New York: Simon & Schuster, 1977.

Clear instructions are given for making a washboard rasp, a washtub bass, and a plastic-bottle banjo.

Lloyd, Norman. "Jazz." In *The Golden Encyclopedia of Music*, 261-270. New York: Golden Press, 1968.

This lengthy article provides a history of jazz from its forerunners to the Modern Jazz Quartet.

Mama Don't Allow. Coproduced by GPN/Nebraska ETV Network and WNED-TV in association with Lancit Media. Reading Rainbow, 30. Lincoln, Nebr.: GPN, [n.d.]. 1 videocassette.

"Mammy Don't 'Low." In *Fireside Book of Fun and Games Songs*, collected and edited by Marie Winn, musical arrangements by Allan Miller, illustrations by Whitney Darrow, Jr., 62. New York: Simon & Schuster, 1974.

McKissack, Patricia, and Frederick McKissack. *Louis Armstrong: Jazz Musician*. Illustrated by Ned O. Great African American Series. Hillside, N.J.: Enslow, 1991.

Born in 1900 in Black Storyville in New Orleans, Louisiana, Armstrong began playing with homemade instruments and later in jazz bands on riverboats.

Newman, Frederick R. *Mouth Sounds: How to Whistle, Pop, Click, and Honk Your Way to Social Success*. Illustrated by Marty Norman, photographs by Jerry Darvin. New York: Workman, 1980.

After an informative introduction on the human voice mechanism, Newman gives instructions on making various sounds with the mouth, including mimicking musical instruments.

DISCOGRAPHY

Armstrong, Louis. *The Legendary Louis Armstrong.* CBS Records, 1990. BT 21727. Sound cassette.

KEYWORDS

Blue notes—in jazz music, scale notes (usually the third and seventh) that have been lowered a half step; this gives the impression of moving into a minor scale, which has a melancholy sound.

Jazz—an American form of music encompassing many styles but based on improvisation and rhythm.

Scat singing—a jazz vocal style in which the vocalist uses nonsense syllables to improvise a melody line in imitation of an instrument.

EXPOSITION

1. Show the students the cover of *Mama Don't Allow* and have them predict where the story takes place and what the plot might be.

2. Ask whether anyone has been on a riverboat or heard a Dixieland band. Talk about New Orleans and the importance of the Mississippi River to its development.

3. As you show the title page, discuss the environment of a swamp.

4. Explain that "Mama Don't Allow" is a song. Ask the students to guess what kind of song (rock 'n roll, folk, classical, jazz) it is.

DEVELOPMENT

1. Read the story, asking individuals to read the balloon sentences spoken by the characters. What kind of voices will they need? Discuss a southern drawl.

2. While singing the song "Mama Don't Allow," accompany yourself on a washboard, vegetable grater, or other homemade instrument. (Use a keyboard if you're unsure of the melody.) Have the students join you.

3. Talk about the fact that American jazz began in New Orleans. Define the term *jazz* and discuss blue notes.

4. Sing or play the song again and see whether the students can detect the blue notes.

5. Introduce Louis Armstrong to the class by sharing information about him from the McKissacks' biography. Emphasize his early experiences with music and discuss his use of scat singing.

6. Play an Armstrong recording that includes an example of scat singing.

RECAPITULATION

1. If available, show the Reading Rainbow video of *Mama Don't Allow.* Discuss the music and how Frederick R. Newman uses his mouth and voice to imitate the instruments.

2. Have the students experiment with mouth sounds and scat singing. Ask them to use sounds and syllables to imitate the instruments.

DEVELOPMENT

1. Read the story. Encourage the students to join in on the refrain, "When a possum come a-knockin' at the door."

2. Establish which words are emphasized or accented (possum, knockin', door). Have the students clap their hands or pat their legs on the strong beats while part of the story is reread.

3. Show the students the "knocks" on the endpapers on the inside of the front and back covers. Define *ostinato*. Assign one group to continue an ostinato of "knock, knock, knock, knock..." while another group chants part of the text. Experiment by trying the ostinato figure only after the refrain.

4. Assign the parts of Granny, Pappy, Ma, and Pa for "What's that?" "Don't know" and "No possum?" "No possum." Reread the story, adding these parts and the ostinato.

RECAPITULATION

1. How does the story end? Who is the narrator? Ask the students for words to describe the possum and its actions.

2. Compare the factual data about opossums from Crofford's *The Opossum* with the fictional characteristics attributed to them by Van Laan.

3. Have the students demonstrate their knowledge of opossums by writing down a physical characteristic on the opossum cut-out pattern in this lesson (see figure 1). Hang the opossums on a paper tree attached either to a bulletin board or to a wall.

4. *Possum Come A-Knockin'* can be staged as a puppet show, with a window frame serving as the stage. Using the figures on the back cover as models, draw the characters on cardboard, cut them out, and attach them to sticks. As each family member is mentioned, the corresponding puppet pops into the window frame.

5. Actors from the class can pantomime activities on one side of a cardboard wall as the possum (in top hat, of course) knocks on the other side. Combine the ostinato and assigned dialogue parts with a choral reading of the book.

CODA

1. Read "Why the Possum's Tail Is Bare" or "Why Possum Has a Naked Tail" as an example of a pourquoi story. Compare these possums' characteristics to those in the Van Laan story. Relate the grinning possum drawn by George Booth to the grinning possum in the pourquoi story you have chosen to read.

3.   As you prepare to reread the story, assign the balloon sentences to individuals and ask for volunteers to imitate the instruments of the Swamp Band as they are introduced in the story.

4.   Showing the students *Emmet Otter's Jug-Band Christmas* and *Simple Folk Instruments to Make and to Play*, discuss ways to make instruments to accompany the song "Mama Don't Allow." Student volunteers can bring in items from home to put together a jug band.

5.   Assemble your own Swamp Band with homemade instruments and voices imitating instruments.

CODA

1.   Because the lyrics of "Mama Don't Allow" could be construed as defiant of authority, try some new lyrics, for example: "Teacher don't allow no bad grammar 'round here.... We care a lot what teacher don't allow. We'll start speaking correctly right now. Teacher doesn't allow any bad grammar around here."

2.   Read *Journey into Jazz* for students to get a feeling for jazz music—its spontaneity yet need for ensemble.

NATHANIEL TALKING

By Eloise Greenfield.
Illustrated by Jan Spivey Gilchrist.
New York: Black Butterfly Children's Books, 1988.

The first poem in this collection is "Nathaniel's Rap," in which Nathaniel explains that he will talk about his philosophy and his "friends and kin" in the rest of the poems.

Lesson grade level: 4 and up

THEME

Using three of the poems in this collection as models, students will write poems in rap and blues patterns.

RESOURCES

Dardick, Geeta. "Born to Sing the Blues." *Cobblestone* 4 (October 1983): 20-23.

This *Cobblestone* issue on jazz features the famous blues singer Bessie Smith, including the words to her "Down-Hearted Blues."

Handy, W. C. "St. Louis Blues." In *Fireside Book of Favorite American Songs*, selected and edited by Margaret Bradford Boni, arranged by Norman Lloyd, illustrated by Aurelius Battaglia, 119-123. New York: Simon & Schuster, 1952.

This well-known blues song follows Greenfield's prescription of three lines of four bars each, with the first two lines being the same.

Hurd, Michael. "Blues." In *The Oxford Junior Companion to Music*, 2nd ed., 64. New York: Oxford University Press, 1979.

This brief explanation of the blues includes a concise definition of the harmonic pattern used in all blues pieces.

KEYWORDS

Blues—a type of jazz music based on African-American work songs that consists of three lines, with the second line a repeat of the first; it is characterized by flatted, or "blue," notes, which give the music its melancholy feeling.

Dominant chord (V chord)—a chord built on the fifth degree of a major or minor scale, for example, G-B-D in the C-major scale.

Rap—to talk rhythmically to the beat of rap music.

Subdominant chord (IV chord)—a chord built on the fourth degree of a major or minor scale, for example, F-A-C in the C-major scale.

Tonic chord (I chord)—a chord built on the first degree of a major or minor scale, for example, C-E-G in the C-major scale.

12-Bar blues—a term describing the musical structure of a blues piece, which is twelve measures long with the following harmonic chord pattern: four measures of the tonic chord (I chord), two measures of the subdominant chord (IV chord), two measures of the tonic, two measures of the dominant chord (V chord) (occasionally the second measure is the subdominant chord), and two measures of the tonic chord.

EXPOSITION

1. Ask the students to explain the word *rap*. Give them one of the slang definitions from the dictionary, which is "talk or conversation." How does this relate to rap music? Discuss what makes rap music different from other rock music. Does rap music tell a story?

2. Show the students the cover of *Nathaniel Talking* and tell them that this book includes a poem that is a rap, another musical form for telling a story.

DEVELOPMENT

1. Read "Nathaniel's Rap." Ask what Nathaniel is rapping about. What do the students think the poems in the book will be about?

2. Read some of the other poems. What do you learn about Nathaniel's family and his feelings about himself and others?

3. Read "My Daddy." Explain that this is the pattern for the words in a blues song. Discuss the word *blues*. Ask the students how they think it got its name.

4. Read the poem again. Ask the students to clap on the beats with you. (Follow Greenfield's division of the beats on the last page of the book.) Explain the term *12-bar blues* and show the students the bar divisions.

5. Print the first verse on the board in three long sentences so the students can see the division of four measures per line.

6. Explain that the 12-bar blues also has a specific harmonic, or chord, pattern. Under the beats, write the chord numbers:

1 2 3 4	1 2 3 4	1 2 3 4	1 2 3 4
I	I	I	I
1 2 3 4	1 2 3 4	1 2 3 4	1 2 3 4
IV	IV	I	I
1 2 3 4	1 2 3 4	1 2 3 4	1 2 3 4
V	V (IV)	I	I

7. On a keyboard, play the following pattern as the students speak the verse (because most beginning piano books have a 12-bar-blues piece, one of the students may be able to play this):

RECAPITULATION

1. Read the poem "Watching the World Go By." Ask the students to write out the verse and divide it into beats.

2. Play the 12-bar-blues chords as the students clap and recite the verse.

3. Ask them what they can do during the long periods of rest at the ends of the lines. Play "St. Louis Blues" or some other blues piece. Point out the embellishment in the piano part when there aren't any words.

4. Try singing "Watching the World Go By" to the tune of "St. Louis Blues." Ask the students to fill in the empty measures with finger snapping and improvised melody.

5. Have the students write their own blues poems. You can start them off with this attempt: "I feel so blue because my teacher makes me work so hard, I feel so blue because my teacher makes me work so hard, I feel like a prisoner with my teacher as the classroom guard."

CODA

1. Read aloud a nonfiction book on the history of the blues or a biography of a blues singer, such as Bessie Smith or "Ma" Rainey, or of blues composer W. C. Handy.

RONDO IN C

By Paul Fleischman.
Illustrated by Janet Wentworth.
New York: Harper & Row, 1988.

As a young girl plays Beethoven's Rondo in C, family and friends describe memories and images triggered by the sounds.

Lesson grade level: 4 and up

THEME

Students will discover the differences between absolute music and program music as they explore the mental images they conjure as they listen to both types of music.

RESOURCES

Beethoven, Ludwig van. "Rondo in C, op. 51, no. 1: For the Piano." New York: G. Schirmer, n.d.

Thompson, Wendy. *Ludwig van Beethoven*. Composer's World. New York: Viking Press, 1990.
    This informative biography includes many paintings of the time period, facsimiles of documents, and full-page excerpts from Beethoven's music.

DISCOGRAPHY

Beethoven, Ludwig van. "Rondo, op. 51, no. 1." Brautigam. Etcetera. XTC-1018. Sound cassette.

Mouret, Jean Joseph. "Rondeau." *TV Classics*. Donald Fraser, English Chamber Orchestra. RCA Victor. BMG Music, 1992. 09026-60935-4. Sound cassette.
    This rondo was popularized as the theme song for the PBS series "Masterpiece Theater."

Saint-Saens, Camille. "Carnival of the Animals." *Classics for Children*. Arthur Fiedler, Boston Pops. RCA (Gold Seal). 6718-4-RG. Sound cassette.

Tchaikovsky, Peter Ilyich. "The Nutcracker Suite." *Classics for Children*. Arthur Fiedler, Boston Pops. RCA (Gold Seal). 6718-4-RG. Sound cassette.

KEYWORDS

Absolute music—music that is written purely for its own sake, in contrast to program music, which tells a story.

Beethoven, Ludwig van (1770-1827)—German composer of the Classical period of music.

Classical music—music composed in the late eighteenth and early nineteenth centuries in Europe.

Key—the tonal center of a piece of music.

Program music—music that describes a particular feeling, mood, scene, story, or idea.

Rondo—a musical form with a repeated refrain alternating with contrasting sections.

EXPOSITION

1. Play a recording of a classical piece that is absolute music. Ask the students to describe in a sentence an image or thought that came to mind.

2. Discuss whether the responses of the students were similar or disparate.

3. Tell the students the name of the piece and ask whether the title has any relation to a thing or place or emotion. (Use a piece that has a form title, such as Prelude, Sonata, Rondo, etc.)

4. Discuss the mood of a piece of music and how its sound can evoke feelings in people. Play examples of music that because of tempo or key sound happy or sad.

DEVELOPMENT

1. Show the book title *Rondo in C* and discuss the rondo form, with its recurring refrain. The pure rondo form is RARBRA'R, in which R is the rondo theme, A and B are contrasting themes, and A' is a variant of the A theme.

2. Read the book. Can the students determine what the music was like by the responses of the characters and corresponding illustrations? Are some thoughts sad, exciting, happy? Could these responses have been triggered by any piece of music?

3. Play a recording of Beethoven's Rondo in C, op. 51, no. 1 or have someone play it on the piano. Ask the students to raise their hands every time they hear the original rondo theme. Discuss the contrasting themes. Can they guess which might match with the characters' thoughts in the book?

4. Show them the musical score and pick out the rondo theme.

5. Explain that this music wasn't written to evoke a particular image or mood and that it is labeled *absolute music*, or music for its own sake.

6. Explain the term *program music*, which tells a story or conjures an assigned image.

7. Play recordings of Saint-Saens's *Carnival of the Animals* or ballet music such as Tchaikovsky's *The Nutcracker*. Point out that the composer had a particular animal or scene in mind when he wrote the music.

RECAPITULATION

1. Play Mouret's "Rondeau." Ask the students to raise their hands when they hear the main theme repeated. How many other themes are included?

2. Play various recordings of classical music. With each piece, ask the stuents to write their first thoughts in complete sentences. If visual images come to mind, ask them to draw them.

3. Divide students into groups and have them discuss their reactions.

4. Intersperse recordings of rondos with other pieces. Ask students to identify which pieces are rondos.

CODA

1. Many pieces of absolute music, such as symphonies and concertos, are later given nicknames by historians. For instance, Beethoven's sixth symphony is called the *Pastoral* Symphony. Have the students examine lists of composers' works for pieces given descriptive names. Find out what the names mean and listen to the music for clues to their origins.

Instruments

All Join In by Quentin Blake

Berlioz the Bear, written and illustrated by Jan Brett

City Sounds by Rebecca Emberley

Good Times on Grandfather Mountain by Jacqueline Briggs Martin

Music, Music for Everyone by Vera B. Williams

Nicholas Cricket by Joyce Maxner

Oh, A-Hunting We Will Go by John Langstaff

ALL JOIN IN

By Quentin Blake.
Boston: Little, Brown, 1990.

With exuberant and wacky pictures, Quentin Blake provides a collection of cacophonous verses glorifying noisy sound.

Lesson grade level: 2 and up

THEME

As they accompany the poem "Sorting Out the Kitchen Pans" on pots and pans of various sizes, students discover that idiophones, or self-sounding instruments, are found everywhere.

RESOURCES

Hurd, Michael. "Idiophone." In *The Oxford Junior Companion to Music*, 184. London: Oxford University Press, 1979.

This brief article lists musical instruments that are idiophones and includes pictures of the means of making idiophones sound.

Kuskin, Karla. "I Woke Up This Morning." In *Dogs and Dragons, Trees and Dreams*, 42-44. New York: Harper & Row, 1980.

As a child is told what to do all day long, her words become larger and larger to match her anger.

Milligan, Spike. "On the Ning Nang Nong." In *The Random House Book of Poetry for Children*, selected and introduced by Jack Prelutsky, illustrated by Arnold Lobel, 171. New York: Random House, 1983.

In this noisy nonsense verse, "cows go bong," "trees go ping," and "mice go clang."

Walther, Tom. "What's an Idiophone?" In *Make Mine Music!*, 56-82. Boston: Little, Brown, 1981.

Beginning with a definition of *idiophone*, Walther describes many idiophones, from rattles to marimbas, providing concise explanations of how the sound is produced and instructions for making these instruments.

KEYWORDS

Cacophony — harsh or discordant sound.

Forte (f) — an Italian musical term indicating a loud dynamic level.

Fortissimo (ff) — a musical term indicating a very loud dynamic level.

Glissando — moving rapidly up or down a series of adjacent notes.

Idiophone ("self-sounding") — a type of percussion instrument that is made from a solid, resonating material that produces sound when struck, shaken, plucked, or rubbed.

Mezzo forte (mf) — a musical term indicating a moderately loud dynamic level.

Mezzo piano (mp) — a musical term indicating a moderately soft dynamic level.

Pianissimo (pp) — a musical term indicating a very soft dynamic level.

Piano (p) — a musical term indicating a soft dynamic level.

EXPOSITION

1. Ask the students for a definition of the word *symphony*. After discussing their answers, point out that the prefix *sym-* means "with" or "together," and the suffix *-phone*, or *phony*, means "sound." Brainstorm other words with *-phone*: *telephone, phonograph,* and *microphone* (refer to a dictionary for word derivations).

2. Bang on some pots and pans and ask the students what kind of sound they are hearing. If you performed successfully, they will say "noise." Write the word *cacophony* on the board and define it. Ask whether this kind of sound is usually soft or loud.

3. Hold up a card with the word *forte* written on it, explaining that the term indicates that the musician should play loudly. Ask how a writer might indicate loudness in a poem (hopefully someone will say that the words are printed in large type).

DEVELOPMENT

1. After discussing the instrumentalist and instrument on the title page of *All Join In*, read the first poem, encouraging the students to shout "All join in!" when you hold up the forte sign.

2. Look at the illustration at the end of the first stanza and have the students identify the instruments. Discuss whether the instruments' sounds would be pleasing or displeasing. Might this be determined by the expectations of the listener? (At this point, depending on the sophistication of the class, you could discuss the attitudes of people toward modern music, in particular, rock music.)

3. Have strips of paper available with the words "Ding, dong, bang" and the other similar phrases from the poem "Sorting Out the Kitchen Pans" written on them. After showing the students the forte words on the page, read the poem and point to the appropriate paper-strip phrases when you want students to join in.

4. Have ten assorted pots and pans available, along with striking implements. Explain that these are idiophones. Separate the word *idiophone* into its two parts. The students should know that *-phone* means "sound." Tell them that *idio-* means "self" or "one's own."

5. Strike each pot and have the class divide them into high, medium, and low sounds. Determine which idiophone will correspond to each word. Do some words sound lower? Does this relate to the vowel sound? Discuss how size and thickness of the material determine the pitch of the idiophone.

RECAPITULATION

1. Assign ten students to ten idiophones, making sure students know the word that corresponds to the sound of their idiophone. Point to each word on the paper strip and have the students practice playing in that sequence.

2. Read the poem again, cuing students with the paper strips. The students without an instrument are the chorus on the line "Sorting out the kitchen pans" whenever it appears. Reread until everyone has had a chance to be in the Cacophony Band.

CODA

1. Have a small group of students read the section on idiophones in *Make Mine Music!* and collect, construct, or report on idiophones.

2. Investigate the range of dynamic signs for music (*pp, p, mp, mf, f,* and *ff*). Prepare the poem "I Woke Up This Morning" by Karla Kuskin as a choral reading. Add voices to represent increases in the sound level.

3. Prepare other poems in *All Join In* by adding a bike horn to "The Hooter Song" and a vocal glissando to the "Wheeee!" in "Sliding."

4. To continue a lesson on vowel sounds and their pitches, use Milligan's poem "On the Ning Nang Nong."

BERLIOZ THE BEAR

Written and illustrated by Jan Brett.
New York: G. P. Putnam's Sons, 1991.

The Berlioz Orchestra is traveling to a Bavarian village for a concert when the mule pulling the bandwagon refuses to budge; help appears in an unexpected form.

Lesson grade level: K to 5

THEME

Using the Berlioz Orchestra as a springboard, the author introduces students to the instruments of an orchestra.

RESOURCES

Berger, Melvin. *The Science of Music*. Illustrated by Yvonne Buchanan. New York: HarperCollins, 1989.

In this exploration of the physics of sound, each instrumental group is examined.

Brett, Jan. "Jan Brett's *Berlioz the Bear*." *Book Links* 1 (November 1991): 50-51.

Jan Brett discusses her inspiration and sources of information for *Berlioz the Bear*.

Hayes, Ann. *Meet the Orchestra*. Illustrated by Karmen Thompson. San Diego, Calif.: Harcourt Brace Jovanovich, 1991.

Ann Hayes provides concise information on each instrument in an orchestra, this one comprising animal musicians.

Kraus, Robert. *Musical Max*. Pictures by Jose Aruego and Ariane Dewey. New York: Simon & Schuster, 1990.

Max plays every instrument, much to the annoyance of neighbors. However, when Max is no longer in the mood and no longer practices, the neighborhood seems too quiet.

Kuskin, Karla. *The Philharmonic Gets Dressed*. Illustrations by Marc Simont. New York: Harper & Row, 1982.

Preparations for an evening concert by the Philharmonic are humorously portrayed as each orchestra member dresses for the occasion.

McMillan, Bruce. *The Alphabet Symphony: An ABC Book*. New York: Greenwillow Books, 1977.

McMillan finds alphabet letters in varied photographic angles of the Portland Symphony Orchestra.

Rubin, Mark. *The Orchestra*. Illustrated by Alan Daniel. Buffalo, N.Y.: Firefly Books, 1984.

Beginning with the rudiments of music, this book discusses each orchestra family and its individual instruments.

Yeoman, John, and Quentin Blake. *Old Mother Hubbard's Dog Learns to Play*. Boston: Houghton Mifflin, 1990.

In this tale told in verse, Old Mother Hubbard wishes her dog would stop reading and "learn how to play." He takes her literally and drives her to distraction playing various musical instruments.

DISCOGRAPHY

Peter Ustinov Reads "The Orchestra." From the book by Mark Rubin. Toronto Philharmonia Orchestra, Walter Babiak. Mark Rubin Productions, 1987. MRP-C107. Sound cassette.

Rimsky-Korsakov, Nicholas. "The Flight of the Bumblebee ." *TV Classics*. Arthur Fiedler, Boston Pops. RCA Victor. BMG Music, 1992. 09026-60935-4. Sound cassette.

KEYWORDS

Band — an instrumental group of mostly brass, woodwind, and percussion instruments.

Berlioz (Ber-lee-oze), Hector (1803-1869) — a French composer noted for his innovative orchestration and his contribution to the development of the modern orchestra.

Encore — a piece played at the end of a concert at the request of the audience.

Largo — an Italian term indicating a very slow musical tempo.

Orchestra — an instrumental group of stringed, brass, woodwind, and percussion instruments.

EXPOSITION

1. Ask the students whether they know what an orchestra is. Discuss the difference between an orchestra and a band.

2. Show the students pictures of instruments (this can be done using posters or charts from encyclopedias) and discuss the names of the instruments and how they are played.

DEVELOPMENT

1. Before reading *Berlioz the Bear*, explain to the students the significance of naming the main character "Berlioz" and give a little background information on the composer. Also note the play on words (*Ber*lioz is a bear).

2. As you read the story, see whether any of the students can determine the instruments from the shapes of the cases in the illustrations. Ask why the Berlioz Orchestra is an orchestra and not a band.

3. Point out the preparations for the concert by the orchestra and by the villagers. Brett's borders include the villagers' activities.

4. At the end of the book play a recording of Rimsky-Korsakov's "Flight of the Bumblebee." Be sure to point out the significance of the mule's name, "Largo," which is printed on the harness.

5. Share the information from Brett's *Book Links* article about modeling the Berlioz Orchestra after the Boston Symphony Orchestra.

6. Read *Musical Max* or *Old Mother Hubbard's Dog Learns to Play* or both for more examples of instruments.

RECAPITULATION

1. Elicit from the students a list of the instruments in the Berlioz Orchestra: double bass, violin, trombone, bass drum, clarinet, and French horn. See whether they can assign them to the correct sections of the orchestra.

2. Listen to the parts of the tape *Peter Ustinov Reads "The Orchestra"* that correspond to the instruments used in *Berlioz the Bear*. Discuss the differences between the sections of the orchestra — the woodwind, brass, string, and percussion sections.

3. Show the photographs in McMillan's *The Alphabet Symphony* and see whether the students can identify the instruments.

4. Assign a section of the orchestra to groups of students. Using *The Orchestra, Meet the Orchestra, The Science of Music*, and encyclopedia sources, have the students prepare an oral report on the various instruments in each section.

CODA

1. Have students bring in recordings of orchestral music from different time periods and discuss the differences in the sound.

2. Arrange to visit a rehearsal by a local orchestra or invite musicians from the orchestra to speak to your class.

3. Make a floor plan of the orchestral sections and discuss the role of the conductor.

4. Read Kuskin's book and have the students compare the preparations of the Philharmonic with those of the Berlioz Orchestra.

CITY SOUNDS

By Rebecca Emberley.
Boston: Little, Brown, 1989.

The onomatopoeic sounds are printed next to the pictures in this noisy tour of a city from sunup to sundown.

Lesson grade level: Pre-K to 2

THEME

All sounds can be approximated by the incredible human voice and then by the written language. Students explore the voice as a resource as they fine-tune their hearing.

RESOURCES

Burningham, John. *Jangle Twang*. Noisy Words. New York: Viking Press, 1985.

This small book of musical instruments has one word on each page to express the sound of the instrument in onomatopoeic fashion.

Emberley, Ed. *Klippity Klop*. Boston: Little, Brown, 1974.

As Prince Krispin and Dumpling leave the castle for an adventure, the horse's hooves make different sounds depending on the material they are crossing.

Emberley, Rebecca. *Jungle Sounds*. Boston: Little, Brown, 1989.

Similar to *City Sounds*, *Jungle Sounds* is filled with onomatopoeic sounds of jungle animals.

Parker, Steve. *Singing a Song: How You Sing, Speak, and Make Sounds*. New York: Franklin Watts, 1991.

With many photographs, this book explains the vocal apparatus and how singing pitches are produced.

Showers, Paul. *The Listening Walk*. Illustrated by Aliki. New York: HarperCollins, 1991.

A "listening walk" with her father requires a little girl to be silent in order to hear the sounds around her.

KEYWORDS

Onomatopoeia—the formation of words that imitate or reproduce sound.

Voice—the sounds produced by the human vocal cords.

EXPOSITION

1. Ask the students to be completely silent and to listen to the sounds around them.

2. Ask individual students to reproduce a sound that they heard.

3. Discuss how some sounds are easier to reproduce than others. Can these sounds be written?

4. Read parts of *The Listening Walk*. Are the animal sounds or the object sounds easier to reproduce?

DEVELOPMENT

1. Go through the book *City Sounds*, pointing at the various pictures and having individual students give interpretations of the sound.

2. Talk about the voice as an instrument and how it makes its sounds. Discuss how most people cannot exactly match the sound of an object or animal but that words can approximate the sound. Discuss the term *onomatopoeia*.

3. Without showing the pictures, say the words in Burningham's *Jangle Twang* and ask the students to name the musical instruments.

RECAPITULATION

1. Assign a sound-producing object to groups of four and ask them to agree on the sound it makes and produce it. For instance, you could distribute a bike bell (*briiing*), a computer keyboard (*clack*), and a pencil sharpener (*whirr*).

2. Have each group share its sounds. Write the approximate words for the sound on chart paper. Ask students to suggest other possibilities. Have the students incorporated different pitches?

3. As a group discuss various settings in which there are many different sounds. Offer suggestions, such as a farm or a restaurant.

4. Using the same groups of students, have them each choose a different setting and practice the sounds related to it. If parent volunteers are available, have each student group work with a parent to record the sounds on tape. Each group then guesses the setting in which the sounds would be heard.

5. As a whole group, pretend that the class is an orchestra. Assign groups of three or four to be various instruments. Have the sections practice their parts using a song melody that everyone knows such as "Jingle Bells" or "Yankee Doodle." Students can also pantomime playing their instruments.

CODA

1. Read *Klippity Klop* and let students try out the sounds the horses's hooves make on the different surfaces. Have small groups say the words that match each surface sound as you reread the book.

2. Take the sounds one step further by asking the students to match each surface sound with that of a rhythm instrument. Read the book again with the rhythm instruments added.

3. Plan and execute a mural of one of the settings, which the students choose. Each student can draw a particular object or action. Label the parts with the approximate sound words.

GOOD TIMES ON GRANDFATHER MOUNTAIN

By Jacqueline Briggs Martin.
Illustrated by Susan Gaber.
New York: Orchard Books, 1992.

After Washburn's cow, pig, and chickens run away, his whittlin' produces new musical uses for the milk bucket, the pig-yard fenceposts, and the chicken-coop door.

Lesson grade level: 3 and up

THEME

Homemade musical instruments were used in pioneer days and are still used in remote sections of rural America. Students learn how to make a few of their own.

RESOURCES

Anderson, Joan. *Pioneer Children of Appalachia*. Photographs by George Ancona. New York: Clarion Books, 1986.

With photographs of Fort New Salem, a living history museum in Salem, West Virginia, Anderson creates a story around the life of a pioneer family in early nineteenth-century Appalachia.

Cline, Dallas. *Homemade Instruments*. New York: Oak, 1976.

Directions are given for making children's instruments based on folk instruments, including a cornstalk fiddle and a willow whistle. Many traditional songs are included.

Hunter, Ilene, and Marilyn Judson. *Simple Folk Instruments to Make and to Play*. New York: Simon & Schuster, 1977.

Instructions are given for making all types of percussion, string, and wind instruments, many requiring only household items.

McLean, Margaret. *Make Your Own Musical Instruments*. Illustrated by Ken Scott. Do It Yourself Books. Minneapolis, Minn.: Lerner, 1988.

Directions are given for making percussion, string, and wind instruments using common materials and, occasionally, tools.

Walter, Mildred Pitts. *Ty's One-Man Band*. Illustrations by Margot Tomes. New York: Scholastic, 1980.

After meeting a man who claims to be a one-man band, Ty gathers a comb, wooden spoons, a tin pail, and a washboard for the evening concert.

KEYWORDS

Clacker—a musical instrument consisting of two blocks of wood that are hit against each other.

Claves—a rhythm instrument comprising two sticks about eight to ten inches long; one stick strikes the other, which is held still.

Corncob whistle—a whistle made out of a hollowed-out corncob.

Guiro—a hollowed-out gourd with a series of indentations that produce a rasping sound when scraped.

Sticks—foot-long wooden cylinders, often grooved, that are played in pairs by striking or scraping.

Tub thumper—a musical instrument like a washtub bass, which consists of an overturned washtub or bucket, a broomstick, and a string or cord connecting the top of the broomstick to the middle of the bucket.

EXPOSITION

1. Ask the students to list the types of materials needed to make various musical instruments. Ask what was used before metals and plastics were available.

2. Show some of the wooden percussion instruments, such as the claves, sticks, and guiro. Discuss how these are made. Could they be made without tools?

3. Explain that many folk instruments were made with simple tools, often from wood.

DEVELOPMENT

1. Read *Good Times on Grandfather Mountain*. As you read, have the students guess what a "clacker" might be. Does the name give you an idea of the sound?

2. At the end of the book, have the students find the instruments on the dance scene page.

3. Using *Simple Folk Instruments to Make and to Play*, show the pictures and instructions for making rhythm sticks and a washtub bass.

4. Have the students brainstorm other kinds of homemade instruments and possible names for them. For instance, two pot lids could be called "clangers." What other instruments might be found around the house?

5. Compare the dancing and instruments of *Good Times on Grandfather Mountain* with those in *Pioneer Children of Appalachia*. Point out the two musical uses of the corn plant: the corncob whistle and the corn-husk fiddle.

RECAPITULATION

1. Discuss the materials available to the pioneer children of Appalachia. This information can be found in Anderson's book.

2. Have the students look through the various homemade-musical-instrument books for instruments that could have been made by pioneer children or children in remote rural areas.

3. After gathering the required materials, have small groups of students make the instruments. (The groups may be determined by the materials the students can provide.)

4. This activity can be incorporated into a unit on colonial America or pioneer days, especially if there are displays or demonstrations of the objects used by the colonists or pioneers.

CODA

1. Read *Ty's One-Man Band* for another example of a simple, inexpensive way to make music.

2. If available, demonstrate the wooden "jumping jack" doll that bounces on a wooden platform to the rhythm of mountain music.

MUSIC, MUSIC FOR EVERYONE

By Vera B. Williams.
New York: Greenwillow Books, 1984.

Rosa and her musical friends form the Oak Street Band to raise money to refill the money jar emptied to buy Rosa's accordion. Their performance at a neighborhood anniversary is enjoyed by the whole community.

Lesson grade level: 2 and up

THEME

Students will determine the role music plays in family and community events as they poll their relatives about musicians and dancing in their family history.

RESOURCES

Ancona, George. *Dancing Is*. New York: E. P. Dutton, 1981.

Ancona's black-and-white photographs capture dances of different ethnic groups, including people of various ages.

Hurd, Michael. "Accordion." In *The Oxford Junior Companion to Music*, 2nd ed., 19. London: Oxford University Press, 1979.

With the help of diagrams, this entry on the accordion describes the various parts of the instrument and how they produce musical sounds.

Lloyd, Norman. "Accordion." In *The Golden Encyclopedia of Music*, 12. New York: Golden Press, 1968.

This entry on the accordion compares it to two similar instruments, the harmonica and the harmonium.

Stadler, John. *Hector the Accordion-Nosed Dog*. Scarsdale, N.Y.: Bradbury Press, 1983.

After smashing into a wall, Hector discovers a new use for his accordion-shaped nose.

Williams, Vera B. *A Chair for My Mother*. New York: Mulberry Books, 1982.

In this book, Rosa and her mother and grandmother are first introduced. After they lose their furniture in a fire, Rosa and her mother and grandmother save dimes in a glass jar to buy a comfortable chair.

_____. *Something Special for Me*. New York: Greenwillow, 1983.

Rosa can't decide what special thing she should buy with her coins from the money jar until she hears a man playing the accordion.

KEYWORDS

Accordion — a wind instrument often called a "squeeze box" that has a keyboard, chord buttons, and a bellows that blows air over reeds.

EXPOSITION

1. Read Williams's *A Chair for My Mother* and *Something Special for Me* or summarize the stories.

2. Discuss the emphasis in these stories on family and community. Compare the neighborhood situation in the books with that of the students. Ask whether they feel a sense of community in their neighborhoods. Do they ever have block parties?

3. Ask the students whether any of their parents, aunts and uncles, or other family members play an instrument or play in a band. (Many students will not be aware of a parent's talents.)

4. Relate to them any of your experiences of music at weddings, reunions, or other events.

DEVELOPMENT

1. Read *Music, Music for Everyone.*

2. Discuss the page borders and how they match what's happening in the illustrations. Are the borders similar on the music-filled pages? Ask the students why this pattern seems musical.

3. Discuss the diversity of the ethnic groups and age levels of the people at the party. Relate the title of the book to the importance of music in gatherings of families or communities.

4. Show the photographs in *Dancing Is* and talk about the events in the pictures. Discuss folk festivals.

RECAPITULATION

1. Have the students take home an interview form that asks family members for information on the role of music in their families. Include questions about the instruments played, types of music played at family gatherings, and favorite dance music.

2. Ask the students to bring in family members' favorite records or sheet music, instruments, and any family photographs of people dancing or playing instruments.

3. Organize a Family Music Fest in which students present their information on the part music plays in their families. Encourage family members to contribute to the oral presentation and play or sing a song.

CODA

1. Read *Hector the Accordion-Nosed Dog* and discuss the mechanics of the accordion.

NICHOLAS CRICKET

By Joyce Maxner.
Illustrated by William Joyce.
New York: HarperCollins, 1989.

Nicholas Cricket and his Bug-a-Wug Band perform nightly for the creatures of the forest and stream in this alliterative poem.

Lesson grade level: 3 and up

THEME

Through *Nicholas Cricket* and other cricket poems, students relate the cricket sound to musical instruments and enjoy rhythmic portrayals of the cricket by various writers.

RESOURCES

Carle, Eric. *The Very Quiet Cricket*. New York: Philomel Books, 1990.

A male cricket meets many animals but doesn't make a sound until he meets a female cricket. Under the final page, a microchip that plays a cricket's sound is a marvelous surprise for reader and listener alike.

Fisher, Aileen. "Halloween Concert." In *Always Wondering: Some Favorite Poems of Aileen Fisher*, drawings by Joan Sandin, 36-37. New York: Harper-Collins, 1991.

A cricket is ready to put down his fiddle and go to sleep for the winter when a field mouse reminds him that it's Halloween and one more concert is required.

Fleischman, Paul. "House Crickets." In *Joyful Noise: Poems for Two Voices*, illustrated by Eric Beddows, 36-38. New York: Harper & Row, 1988.

Two crickets living under the gas stove observe the passing of the seasons by the type of food dropped on the floor.

Hogner, Dorothy Childs. *Grasshoppers and Crickets*, 43-58. Illustrated by Nils Hogner. New York: Thomas Y. Crowell, 1960.

This book gives a concise description of the "singing" apparatus of a common cricket and discusses the cricket's use in China as a good-luck charm.

Jacobson, Lois. "Keeping Cool with Crickets." *Cricket* 19 (August 1992): 25-27.

After a Westerner staying in Tokyo for the summer receives a welcome gift of a cricket water dish, she buys a cricket and a bamboo cage. Her neighbor explains her gift by saying she must "learn to keep cool with crickets."

Keats, Ezra Jack. *Maggie and the Pirate*. New York: Four Winds Press, 1979.

Maggie keeps her pet cricket in a cricket cage until a "pirate" steals the cage and a disaster occurs.

KEYWORDS

Banjo — a stringed instrument with a long neck and a round, parchment-covered frame used widely in American folk music.

Kazoo — an instrument that consists of a tube or pipe covered at one end with a thin material over which a person hums or sings, producing a nasal tone.

EXPOSITION

1. Read Carle's *The Very Quiet Cricket*. Discuss the cricket's sound at the end of the book. Does it sound real? Ask the students when and where they have heard crickets.

2. Using the factual information about crickets in Carle's book and in nonfiction books, discuss how the cricket makes its sound.

3. Ask the students to describe the sound. Can they relate it to that of a musical instrument?

DEVELOPMENT

1. Discuss the cover picture of *Nicholas Cricket*. Ignoring the fact that the characters are insects, discuss the style of Nick's clothing. (Some may notice the similarity between Nick's clothing and Dick Tracy's.)

2. Talk about the banjo and the type of music that is associated with it.

3. Read *Nicholas Cricket*, emphasizing the rhyming and alliterative sounds. Have the students join in on "The music is just so grand."

4. Because the pictures are dark, allow the students time to locate the various insects and animals mentioned in the book.

5. Have the students recall the instruments mentioned. Read again the descriptions of the "washboard strummers," "slap-a-spoon drummers," and the "crick-crick-crickety kazoo hummers." Find these instruments in the illustrations.

RECAPITULATION

1. Read Fisher's poem "Halloween Concert." What instrument does the cricket play? What does this poem tell you about a cricket's habits as winter approaches? How does this concert compare with the Bug-a-Wug Band's? Can the students discern a difference in musical style?

2. Read Fleischman's "House Crickets" with another person. Be sure to pronounce the word *cricket* so it sounds like a cricket and be sure the two voices are synchronized.

3. Using rhythm instruments, washboards, spoons, and kazoos, have the students orchestrate an accompaniment to the reading of *Nicholas Cricket*. The kazoos can approximate the cricket sound made by the microchip in Carle's book.

4. Combine the reading of *Nicholas Cricket* with the other poems for a Cricket Concert.

CODA

1. Use this program as part of a culmination of an insect unit.

2. Using *Maggie and the Pirate* as an introduction, discuss the use of the cricket as a good-luck charm. Show pictures of cricket cages and have the students make some out of toothpicks.

3. Read "Keeping Cool with Crickets" and discuss the use of crickets in Japan.

4. Supply the students with cardboard and pipe cleaners and have them construct Nick's Cafe, the musicians, instruments, and dancers.

OH, A-HUNTING WE WILL GO

By John Langstaff.
Pictures by Nancy Winslow Parker.
New York: Aladdin Books, 1991.

Langstaff and friends (see dedication) have expanded the original folk song to include many animals who are put in various places and then let go.

Lesson grade level: K and up

THEME
Students learn the history of the modern-day horn as they investigate the hunting horn and make a simple horn.

RESOURCES
Ardley, Neil. "Beginning of Brass." In *Music*, 20-21. Eyewitness Books. New York: Alfred A. Knopf, 1989.

This two-page spread with photographs and brief descriptions shows early horns such as the Roman cornu, the post horn, and the eighteenth-century horn with crooks.

Berger, Melvin. "Brasses." In *The Science of Music*, illustrated by Yvonne Buchanan, 102-108. New York: HarperCollins, 1989.

This section provides a history of horns and an explanation of how the mechanism and musicians interact to make the sound.

Hunter, Ilene, and Marilyn Judson. *Simple Folk Instruments to Make and to Play*, 154. New York: Simon & Schuster, 1977.

Directions are given for making a "Plastic Tube Horn" using a plastic tube, a funnel, and a mouthpiece from a brass instrument or a whistle.

Hurd, Michael. "Horns and the Horn Family." In *The Oxford Junior Companion to Music*, 178. London: Oxford University Press, 1979.

"The Noble Duke of York." In *Jim Along, Josie: A Collection of Folk Songs and Singing Games for Young Children*, compiled by Nancy Langstaff and John Langstaff, illustrated by Jan Pienkowski, 90-91. New York: Harcourt Brace Jovanovich, 1970.

Wiseman, Ann. *Making Musical Things: Improvised Instruments*, 37. New York: Charles Scribner's Sons, 1979.

Directions are given for making a horn out of shower hose, a shower bulb (head), and a tin funnel.

KEYWORDS
Embouchure (am-boo-shoor)—the position and shape of the mouth, lips, and tongue needed to play a true pitch on a woodwind instrument.

Hunting horn—a metal instrument consisting of a coiled tube with a "bell" on one end and a mouthpiece on the other.

Kazoo—an instrument that consists of a tube or pipe covered at one end with a thin material over which a person hums or sings, producing a nasal tone.

Overtones—softened tones produced by portions of a string or column of air vibrating at the same time as the predominant tone produced by the vibration of the entire string or column of air. The frequencies of these tones are exact multiples of the frequency of the predominant tone. Overtones on a horn are produced by overblowing.

Post horn—a brass instrument consisting of a straight or coiled tube capable of playing only a single note and its overtones; used for signaling mail coaches.

Reveille (revelly)—a military signal played at the start of the day, usually on a bugle.

EXPOSITION

1. Show the students Langstaff's title page with the hunting horn. Discuss the use of the horn in hunting foxes.

2. Discuss the history of the horn, using the resources listed above. Mention the use of the horn by postal workers. If you can find a picture of a mailbox with a horn on it, bring it in. They are often available in mail-order catalogues.

3. Demonstrate the parts of a hunting horn by coiling plastic tubing and putting a funnel on one end to represent the bell.

4. By placing a kazoo in the tubing as a mouthpiece, you can play reveille before you read the book.

DEVELOPMENT

1. As you read the book, point out the various apparatuses that the children are carrying. Have the students guess where the animal will be put.

2. Have the students sing along on "Oh, a-hunting we will go."

3. Ask the students whether they know another song with the same melody. Some will recognize the tune as "The Noble Duke of York."

4. Using pictures, compare the hunting horn to the modern French horn. Discuss the limited notes the coiled horn can play. Using Berger's book, explain the use of embouchure to change notes. Discuss the use of crooks to change the length of the tube and how this expanded the horn's ability to produce notes.

5. If possible, have someone come in to demonstrate the French horn and explain the way different tones are produced.

RECAPITULATION

1. Ask students to bring in kazoos or have some available.

2. Divide the class into groups of six, with a kazoo owner in each group.

3. Have each group come up with two new verses, along with illustrations of the animals in the containers. If the animal topic seems to be exhausted, try people: "catch a teacher and put her in a bleacher."

4. Lend the tubing and bell in turn to each kazoo player and have each group sing their verses and display their pictures to the rest of the class.

CODA

1. Once the song is learned, try different beginnings, such as "A-writing we will go, a-writing we will go, we'll pick a noun and make it a clown and then we'll have a show." (The students will think of better ones.)

2. Sing "The Noble Duke of York" with the accompanying actions.

Dances

Barn Dance by Bill Martin, Jr., and John Archambault

The Dancing Granny, retold and illustrated by Ashley Bryan

Dancing the Breeze by George Shannon

Dinosaur Dances by Jane Yolen

Mirandy and Brother Wind by Patricia C. McKissack

Shimmy Shake Earthquake: Don't Forget to Dance Poems, collected and illustrated by Cynthia Jabar

Skip to My Lou, adapted and illustrated by Nadine Bernard Westcott

BARN DANCE

By Bill Martin, Jr., and John Archambault.
Illustrated by Ted Rand.
New York: Henry Holt, 1986.

A sleepless boy is drawn to the barn by a fiddle's "plink plink" and joins the farm animals in a hoedown.

Lesson grade level: Pre-K and up

THEME

Using the rhythm and square-dance calls of *Barn Dance*, students learn simple square-dance steps.

RESOURCES

DeFelice, Cynthia C. *The Dancing Skeleton*. Illustrated by Robert Andrew Parker. New York: Macmillan, 1989.

Aaron Kelly came back from the grave, turned into a skeleton, and refused to go away until a fiddle tune made him dance till all his bones fell in a heap.

Hammond, Mildred. *Square Dancing Is for Me*. Minneapolis, Minn.: Lerner, 1983.

With photographs of children demonstrating the steps, simple square-dance patterns are explained.

McLoughland, Beverly. "Bird Barn Dance." *Ranger Rick* 22 (November 1988): 20.

Numerous bird names appear in this poem written with a square-dance rhythm.

Nevell, Dick. "Cowboy Dances." *Cobblestone* 3 (July 1982): 30-33.

Nevell traces the historical path of this dance form from colonial American country dances to cowboy dances, or square dances. With calls and diagrams, he describes "The Gal from Arkansas," a popular dance of the Old West that can be danced to "Yankee Doodle."

Seeger, Ruth Crawford (comp.). "Old Joe Clarke." In *American Folk Songs for Children, in Home, School, and Nursery School: A Book for Children, Parents, and Teachers*, illustrated by Barbara Cooney, 84-85. New York: Doubleday, 1948.

This fast-moving folk song is a perfect accompaniment for a square dance.

"Turkey in the Straw." In *Fireside Book of Folk Songs*, selected and edited by Margaret Bradford Boni, arranged for the piano by Norman Lloyd, illustrated by Alice Provensen and Martin Provensen, 66. New York: Simon & Schuster, 1947.

This is a favorite fiddle tune for square dancing.

DISCOGRAPHY

Copland, Aaron. "Rodeo: Hoedown." *Copland — Greatest Hits*. Arthur Fiedler, Boston Pops. RCA Victor. BMG Music, 1991. 60837-4-RG. Sound cassette.

KEYWORDS

Do-si-do (do-sa-do) — square dance step in which a person walks around his or her partner, going forward past the right shoulder and backwards past the left shoulder.

Hoedown — an informal dancing party that features square dancing.

Square dance — a set dance usually performed by four couples arranged to form a hollow square.

EXPOSITION

1. Play a recording of square-dance music, such as Copland's "Rodeo," or play "Turkey in the Straw" or "Old Joe Clarke" on a keyboard. Ask the students to identify the type of music and to determine the instruments if a recording is used.

2. Explain that fiddles and banjos are played at hoedowns. Discuss the square dance and the calls that are used.

3. Ask the students why hoedowns are held in barns.

DEVELOPMENT

1. Read *Barn Dance* as rhythmically as possible, slowing down at the end as the boy starts back to his room.

2. Encourage the students to clap to the rhythm of the square-dance calls that are italicized. Go over these a couple of times and examine the illustrations for the dance steps the animals are doing.

3. Using *Square Dancing Is for Me*, teach the patterns mentioned in the book and other basic patterns. Have the students speculate on the phrases that are unknown, such as "rocket to the moon an' powder-puff your noses."

4. As you read the dance section again, have pairs of students arranged in a square try out the steps.

RECAPITULATION

1. Read the instructions for "The Gal from Arkansas" in *Cobblestone*. Have the students walk through the steps. After they feel comfortable with the order of the steps, play "Yankee Doodle" and try them to music.

2. Read "Bird Barn Dance." Have the students clap along with the rhythm of the poem. Read each verse slowly and ask the students whether they can think of square-dance steps to match the words.

3. Divide students into groups of eight and have each group plan a square dance for the poem.

4. Perform each dance, with one group clapping the rhythm as the poem is read.

CODA

1. Read *The Dancing Skeleton* and discuss the rhythmic rhyming phrases such as "crickety-crack, down and back."

2. Plan a performance of this story with accompaniment on rhythm instruments that sound like bones.

THE DANCING GRANNY

Retold and illustrated by Ashley Bryan.
New York: Atheneum, 1977.

Spider Ananse of African folklore tricks Granny into dancing away from her garden so he can take her vegetables, only to be drawn into the dance himself.

Lesson grade level: 3 and up

THEME

After an introduction to the chant "Shake it to the east..." in *The Dancing Granny*, students learn the song "Little Sally Walker," which uses the four notes of the chant "allee allee in free." Students also compare the trickster tales from the African-American and Native-American cultures and discuss the value of shared stories.

RESOURCES

Goble, Paul. *Iktomi and the Boulder: A Plains Indian Story*. New York: Orchard Books, 1988.

In a Native-American tale of how the Plains became littered with rocks, Iktomi, the Plains Indian trickster, must use all his powers to escape a boulder that is chasing him.

Hunter, Ilene, and Marilyn Judson. *Simple Folk Instruments to Make and to Play*. New York: Simon & Schuster, 1977.

Kimmel, Eric A. *Anansi and the Moss-Covered Rock*. Illustrated by Janet Stevens. New York: Holiday House, 1988.

Anansi, the trickster spider, uses the magic powers of a moss-covered rock to steal the jungle animals' food until a little deer uses the same trick to outwit him.

"Little Sally Walker." In *Shake It to the One That You Love the Best: Play Songs and Lullabies from Black Musical Traditions*, collected and adapted by Cheryl Warren Mattox, with illustrations from the works of Varnette P. Honeywood and Brenda Joysmith, 8. El Sobrante, Calif.: Warren-Mattox Productions, 1989.

In this African-American game song, children stand in a ring and rhythmically chant "Shake it to the east..." with accompanying motions.

Merriam, Eve. "Snow in the East." In *You Be Good & I'll Be Night*. New York: Morrow Junior Books, 1988.

Patterned after "Shake it to the east," there is a verse for snow, grass, rain, light, and night.

KEYWORDS

Calabash — an idiophone of African descent consisting of a hollow gourd with beads strung on the outside.

G-E-A-G-E — notes to the children's universal sing-song tease based on a series of overtones in the harmonic scale.

Overtones — softened tones produced by portions of a string or column of air vibrating at the same time as the predominant tone produced by the vibration of the entire string or column of air. The frequencies of these tones are exact multiples of the frequency of the predominant tone.

EXPOSITION

1. Introduce or review the character of Anansi the Spider from African folklore. Ask the students to describe him (for example, lazy, tricky, hungry).

2. Discuss why the students think this character is popular in African folklore and relate him to the coyote and Iktomi in Native-American stories.

3. Explain that the character of Anansi (Ananse) the Spider appears often in West-Indian stories under the name Aunt Nancy.

DEVELOPMENT

1. Teach the students the verse "Shake it to the east...." Some may know it as a jump-rope chant.

2. Explain that *The Dancing Granny* is a folktale from the West Indies. Read the story, asking the students to join in on "Shake it to the east...."

3. Introduce the calabash and add it to the refrain.

4. Teach the song "Little Sally Walker" from Mattox's book. Ask the students whether they recognize the melodic pattern of the phrase "Little Sally Walker." Explain that it is a pattern common throughout the Western world. They may know the words "allee allee in free."

RECAPITULATION

1. Explore the similarities and differences of the trickster characters from the African tradition and the Native-American tradition, using *Anansi and the Moss-Covered Rock* and *Iktomi and the Boulder*.

2. Discuss with the students the cultural values that are promoted in a folktale. Can they determine the values from the three trickster stories?

3. Dividing into groups, practice and perform the three stories in a readers theatre production of trickster stories. Have the students add appropriate rhythm instruments to the readings, such as the calabash or Native-American rattles.

4. Using the preface of *Shake It to the One That You Love the Best*, lead the students in a discussion of culture and heritage. Use the term *cultural literacy* and discuss the value of shared cultural knowledge.

5. Investigate the rest of the songs in *Shake It to the One That You Love the Best* to find out which are familiar to the students. Are the melodies exactly the same as the ones the students know? Discuss the oral tradition and the reasons for variations in song and stories.

CODA

1. Have the students pick the songs and dances they want to learn from *Shake It to the One That You Love the Best*. Perform these for other classes.

2. Teach Merriam's poem "Snow in the East." Using the pattern of this poem, have each child write a stanza for a class poem.

3. Using *Simple Folk Instruments to Make and to Play*, show the students how to make a calabash. Instructions for making a calabash from a hollow gourd strung with wooden or glass beads are given on pages 48-49. If a gourd is not available, try stringing the beads on a papier-mâché form.

DANCING THE BREEZE

By George Shannon.
Pictures by Jacqueline Rogers.
New York: Bradbury Press, 1991.

A father and child dance the breeze dance with the flowers in the garden as dusk turns to evening.

Lesson grade level: Pre-K to 2

THEME

Students move to quarter notes or eighth notes, depending on the size of the dancing flower they choose.

RESOURCES

"The Bear Went over the Mountain." In *Singing Bee! A Collection of Favorite Children's Songs*, compiled by Jane Hart, pictures by Anita Lobel, 112. New York: Lothrop, Lee & Shepard Books, 1982.

Eastwick, Ivy O. "The Stars, the Dark, and the Daisies." In *When the Dark Comes Dancing: A Bedtime Poetry Book*, compiled by Nancy Larrick, 26. New York: Philomel Books, 1983.

When the dark dances over the daisies, they tuck in their heads, but when the stars dance over, the daisies join the dance.

Lobel, Anita. *Alison's Zinnia*. New York: Greenwillow Books, 1990.

In this flower alphabet, the name of the girl matches the alphabet letter of the flower, which is given to a girl whose name begins with the next letter in the alphabet. (Thus, Alison acquired an amaryllis for Beryl, and Alison received a zinnia from Zelda.)

DISCOGRAPHY

Tchaikovsky, Peter Ilyich. "The Nutcracker." *Classics for Children*. Arthur Fiedler. Boston Pops. RCA (Gold Seal). 6718-4-RG. Sound cassette.

KEYWORDS

Eighth note—in 3/4 meter, a note with a duration of a half beat.

Quarter note—in 3/4 meter, a note with a duration of one beat.

EXPOSITION

1. Begin with a flower seed catalog or seed packets. Talk about the various names of the flowers and their colors. Discuss and compare their various sizes.

2. Ask the students how various flowers would move. What would make a flower move? How would a long stalk, large petals, or skinny leaves affect the movement?

3. Ask whether the students have heard the breeze. What is a breeze like? How does it differ from a gale?

DEVELOPMENT

1. Read *Dancing the Breeze*. Ask the students to listen for the words that describe sounds and movements.

2. After reading the book, ask what the "old dry leaves" sounded like.

3. Which flowers danced with long steps and which with short steps? Go through the book again and list the flowers under "Long" and "Short." Look at pictures of other flowers, using the catalogs and *Alison's Zinnia*. Add some of these flowers to the lists.

4. Ask a few students to pretend they are the long flowers and to move to the beat as you play steady quarter-note beats at a moderate tempo using a keyboard or drum. Discuss how long a stride they need to fill the beat's duration.

5. Next choose students to move as the short flowers. Keep the same tempo but play eighth notes instead, so there are twice as many drum beats. The short flowers should not move farther; they should simply take smaller steps.

RECAPITULATION

1. Have each student choose a flower. Divide the students into "Long" and "Short" groups. Give the groups paper in a size that corresponds to their beat length. The quarter-note paper will be twice as long as the eighth-note paper.

2. Have the students draw their flowers with stem and leaves, filling the sheet of paper.

3. Practice with each group until members can move to their respective beats. Switch back and forth and see whether both groups can continue their stride.

4. The students can hold their flowers as they move. Eventually, make a flower garden on the wall.

CODA

1. Read the poem, "The Stars, the Dark, and the Daisies" and discuss the images. Why would the flowers dance under the stars and not under the dark?

2. This poem can be sung to the tune "The Bear Went over the Mountain." The students can sing this while moving around the room with their dancing flowers. Allow free movement on this poem.

3. Play a recording of "The Waltz of the Flowers" from *The Nutcracker Suite* and have the students dance with their flowers.

DINOSAUR DANCES

By Jane Yolen.
Illustrated by Bruce Degen.
New York: G. P. Putnam's Sons, 1990.

Seventeen poems describe the various dinosaur dances at a prehistoric party of the Cretaceous period.

Lesson grade level: 1 to 3

THEME
Students realize the importance and variety of meters in dance forms.

RESOURCES
Allen, Linda. "Mrs. Simkin and the Groovy Old Gramophone." *Cricket* 19 (June 1992): 44-49.

When Mrs. Simkin tries out her Granny's old gramophone, it plays old-fashioned dance tunes all day for Mr. and Mrs. Simkin and the neighbors, ending with a conga line at midnight.

Kuskin, Karla. "A Dance." In *Dogs & Dragons, Trees & Dreams*, 12-13. New York: Harper & Row, 1980.

With a strong rhythm and dancing terms, Kuskin takes us on a wild dance, ending with "a man in a mustache is wearing my shoe."

Lloyd, Norman. "Polka." In *The Golden Encyclopedia of Music*, 432-433. New York: Golden Press, 1968.

This article describes and cites the origins of the polka and provides illustrations of its steps.

Lloyd, Norman. "Tango." In *The Golden Encyclopedia of Music*, 584. New York: Golden Press, 1968.

The tango is explained with rhythmic notation, an illustration, and a written description of the steps.

"The Man on the Flying Trapeze." In *An Illustrated Treasury of Songs*, compiled by the National Gallery of Art, 68-69. Milwaukee, Wis.: Hal Leonard; New York: Rizzoli, 1991.

"The Noble Duke of York." In *Singing Bee! A Collection of Favorite Children's Songs*, compiled by Jane Hart, pictures by Anita Lobel, 88. New York: Lothrop, Lee & Shepard Books, 1982.

Shannon, George. *Dance Away*. Illustrated by Jose Aruego and Ariane Dewey. New York: Mulberry Books, 1982.

Rabbit's friends begin to hide from him to avoid his constant dancing. However, in the end, his "left two three kick" saves the day.

KEYWORDS
3/4—a time signature indicating three beats in a measure of music, with the quarter note receiving one beat.

4/4—a time signature indicating four beats in a measure of music, with the quarter note receiving one beat.

Conga—a Cuban dance of African origins that consists of a line of people following a leader and dancing a pattern of three steps and a kick.

Measure—in musical notation, a group of musical beats separated by bar lines.

Meter—the arrangement of beats into groups of equal size, with a defined pattern of accented and unaccented beats.

KEYWORDS—(*Continued*)

Polka—a couple dance in 2/4 meter with the following rhythm:

Tango—a ballroom dance from Central America and Argentina that features gliding steps interrupted by sudden stops and follows this rhythm:

Waltz—a dance for couples in 3/4 meter.

EXPOSITION

1. Because this lesson would probably be used during a study of dinosaurs and prehistoric times, a quick review of the various dinosaurs would be all that is needed to introduce the lesson.

2. Have the students list types of dances that they know.

3. Show the students *Dinosaur Dances* and ask whether they can imagine a dinosaur dancing.

4. Read the first poem, "Dinosaur Dances," as an introduction.

DEVELOPMENT

1. Read "A Dance" by Karla Kuskin. Have the students clap on the strong beats. There are either two or four beats in a line.

2. Discuss the importance of meter in dances. Demonstrate by playing or singing a waltz and a march piece and having the students clap the number of beats. (Use "The Man on the Flying Trapeze" for the waltz and "The Noble Duke of York" for the march.)

3. Ask them to clap louder on the strong beats. Then determine the total beats in a measure in the waltz (3/4 meter) and the march (4/4 meter).

4. Ask what would happen to partners in a dance if the number of beats kept changing.

RECAPITULATION

1. Read the first verse of Yolen's "Dinosaur Waltz" from chart paper onto which you have copied the poem. Have the students determine the accented words or syllables. Clap on the strong beats and sing the poem to the melody of "The Man on the Flying Trapeze."

2. Read Yolen's poem "Square Dance" and ask the students to clap on the beats. This meter is 4/4 (four beats to a line).

3. Read Yolen's poem "When the Allosaurus" and have the students pick out the names of the dances.

4. Divide the students into groups and, using music encyclopedias and general encyclopedias, have each group research a dance and report on its origins, meter, and dance steps and provide musical titles for that type of dance.

CODA

1. Read Allen's "Mrs. Simkin and the Groovy Old Gramophone." Discuss the dances listed, especially the conga.

2. Read Shannon's *Dance Away* as another example of the conga line.

3. At the end of the lesson, lead the students in a conga line.

MIRANDY AND BROTHER WIND

By Patricia C. McKissack.
Illustrated by Jerry Pinkney.
New York: Alfred A. Knopf, 1988.

Mirandy tries various methods to capture Brother Wind for her dance partner at the cakewalk.

Lesson grade level: 2 and up

THEME

In learning about the cakewalk and its accompanying music, the students will "conjure" their own wind character and imagine its music.

RESOURCES

Debussy, Claude. "Golliwogg's [sic] Cake-Walk." In *Easy Piano Classics*, (compiled by) Philip Hawthorn, edited by Jenny Tyler and Helen Davies, music arrangements by Daniel Scott, 58. Usborne Learn to Play. Tulsa, Okla.: EDC, 1990.

This simplified piano arrangement still gives the flavor of the syncopated rhythm.

———. "Golliwog's Cake-Walk." In *Children's Corner for Piano*. New York: Carl Fischer, 1983.

Hitchcock, H. Wiley, and Stanley Sadie, eds. "Cakewalk." In *The New Grove Dictionary of American Music*, 343. London: Macmillan, 1986.

This entry explains the origins of the cakewalk, a description of the dance, and the music associated with it.

Mills, Kerry. "At a Georgia Camp Meeting." In *Fireside Book of Favorite American Songs*, selected and edited by Margaret Bradford Boni, arranged for the piano by Norman Lloyd, illustrated by Aurelius Battaglia, 47. New York: Simon & Schuster, 1952.

This march/two-step piece, popularized by Sousa's band in 1898, was a cakewalk accompaniment.

Preston, Catherine. *Scott Joplin*, 48-50. Black Americans of Achievement. New York: Chelsea House, 1988.

This section of the ragtime composer's biography shows a photograph of cakewalk dancers and provides a description and history.

Rosetti, Christina. "Who Has Seen the Wind?" In *Windy Day: Stories and Poems*, edited by Caroline Feller Bauer, illustrated by Dirk Zimmer, xiii. New York: J. B. Lippincott, 1988.

This poem describes how the wind can be seen in the objects it moves.

DISCOGRAPHY

Debussy, Claude. "Golliwog's Cakewalk." *Johanna Harris: A Living Legacy*. Johanna Harris. MCA Classics. MCAC-6260. Sound cassette.

KEYWORDS

Cakewalk — a nineteenth-century dance arising from African-American culture, characterized by high-stepping and strutting couples in a grand-march formation.

Debussy, Claude (1862-1918) — a French composer who founded the musical style *impressionism*, which evoked subtle moods or impressions.

Golliwog — a black rag doll.

EXPOSITION

1. Read Rosetti's poem "Who Has Seen the Wind?" Have the students describe the wind and its movements. Discuss how we "see" the wind by the objects it moves.

2. Explain that Mirandy in *Mirandy and Brother Wind* wants the wind as a dance partner. What kind of dance can the students envision for the wind? Is it a tango, a waltz, a bunny hop?

DEVELOPMENT

1. Read *Mirandy and Brother Wind*. Explain terms such as *conjure* and *do your biddin'* as you read. Periodically check the students' comprehension of Mirandy and Ezel's relationship.

2. Discuss the illustrator's conception of Brother Wind. Is the wind depicted differently in other stories or rhymes? Ask the students to describe the North Wind.

3. Tell the students that Jerry Pinkney used himself as a model for Brother Wind. (He revealed this in a 1991 Friends of the Denver Public Library luncheon speech.)

4. Describe the cakewalk and explain the origin of the name.

5. Compare photographs of the cakewalk in *The New Grove Dictionary of American Music* or *Scott Joplin* with Pinkney's painting. Is his illustration accurate?

RECAPITULATION

1. Play a march or two-step such as Mills's "At a Georgia Camp Meeting." How would Brother Wind move to this music? Explain that this music was used for cakewalks, as were ragtime pieces.

2. Discuss the march tempo and have the students envision the high-stepping promenade.

3. Play a recording of Debussy's "Golliwog's Cakewalk." Ask the students to describe the music. Is it flowing or halting? Explain that the golliwog was a rag doll. How would its cakewalk differ from that of the wind?

4. Give the students crayons or collage materials and ask them to draw or construct a mask of a wind character. (Supply as many scarves as you can.) Can they match the character to a specific dance?

CODA

1. Because the cakewalk was originally a contest with a cake as the prize, organize a carnival cakewalk with cupcakes as prizes.

2. Play the tape of "Golliwog's Cakewalk" and have the students step to the beat.

SHIMMY SHAKE EARTHQUAKE:
DON'T FORGET TO DANCE POEMS

Collected and illustrated by Cynthia Jabar.
Boston: Little, Brown, 1992.

Celebrating dance and movement, this collection of eighteen poems is alive with snappy rhythms and action-filled words.

Lesson grade level: Pre-K and up

THEME

These poems will help students lose inhibitions and activate craziness as they experience the joy of moving to poetry. The activities are ideal for pairing "buddies" from a primary and an intermediate grade.

RESOURCES

Larrick, Nancy. "Moving into Poetry." In *Let's Do a Poem! Introducing Poetry Through Listening, Singing, Chanting, Impromptu Choral Reading, Body Movement, Dance, and Dramatization*, 65-84. New York: Delacorte Press, 1991.

Beginning with action games, Larrick continues with poems that suggest movement and, finally, poems that seem to require movement.

Raffi. "Shake My Sillies Out." In *The Book of Kids Songs: A Holler-Along Handbook*, by Nancy Cassidy and John Cassidy, illustrated by Jim M'Guinness, music produced by Ken Whiteley, 24. Palo Alto, Calif.: Klutz Press, 1986.

Acting out this song is a good way to loosen kids up to try dance movements, for they are instructed to clap, jump, yawn, stretch, and shake. (Comes with a cassette tape.)

KEYWORDS

Boogie — energetic dancing to rock music.

Bugaloo — a dance for couples who dance apart, moving to the beat with short, quick movements.

Fandango — a Spanish dance of three or six beats to a measure that is characterized by an increasing tempo and sudden, motionless stops.

Lindy — a jitterbug dance; its name is probably derived from Charles Lindbergh's nickname, "Lindy."

Polonaise — a stately Polish dance with strong accents.

EXPOSITION

1. Ask the students how many of them like to dance. What kinds of dances do they do? See whether anyone will demonstrate.

2. Why do people dance? Ask whether they ever find themselves tapping their feet and wanting to dance when they hear music.

3. Show the endpapers of *Shimmy Shake Earthquake*. Can the students recognize the dances?

4. Discuss the title and ask for demonstrations of a "shimmy shake." Try your own interpretation, especially if the students seem inhibited. Point out the subtitle.

DEVELOPMENT

1. Read "I can do the cancan." Ask students to demonstrate the dances listed. If they don't know them, show them. Ask for seven volunteers to pantomime a line apiece of the poem while you recite it.

2. Next read "B Boy." Ask the students to provide a rap accompaniment.

3. Try "Shimmy Shake It!" and see whether some brave volunteers will dance to the poem.

4. Explain that many poems invite movement because of their strong rhythm and the movement words that the poets use.

5. Read "Forty Performing Bananas" and ask the students to keep track of the dance names or dance movements they hear. Ask them to try to imagine bananas doing these movements.

RECAPITULATION

1. Inform the students that they will be performing the poems in the book. Prepare them for the experience by reading "Fancy Dancer." Discuss how the dancer takes chances and keeps trying.

2. To warm up physically, play the recording "Shake My Sillies Out" and encourage the students to move around as they sing.

3. Divide the class into as many groups as there are poems you would like to perform. "Forty Performing Bananas" and "Tap-Dancing" will need large groups. Not all the poems need to be performed. Some are easier to choreograph than others.

4. Encourage the older students to look up a particular dance in the dictionary or encyclopedia if they are unfamiliar with it. (Other teachers can be a great resource, too.)

5. In a paired situation, the older students read the poems while the younger ones perform. Encourage the use of costumes or props and the use of taped background music.

CODA

1. With the older students, examine other poetry anthologies for more examples of poems that invite movement.

SKIP TO MY LOU

Adapted and illustrated by Nadine Bernard Westcott.
Boston: Little, Brown, 1989.

In this humorous picture book of the American folk song, a small boy left in charge of the farm is joined in a dance by the farm animals, beginning with "flies in the sugarbowl."

Lesson grade level: Pre-K and up

THEME

Reliving the play parties of American pioneers, students dance to "Skip to My Lou" and learn the song by identifying the similar phrases.

RESOURCES

Seeger, Ruth Crawford (comp.). "Skip-a to My Lou." In *American Folk Songs for Children in Home, School, and Nursery School: A Book for Children, Parents, and Teachers*, illustrated by Barbara Cooney, 166-167. Garden City, N.Y.: Doubleday, 1948.

Seeger's version has different melodic lines for the verse and chorus and includes twenty-two verse variants.

"Skip to My Lou." In *Go In and Out the Window: An Illustrated Songbook for Young People*, music arranged and edited by Dan Fox, commentary by Claude Marks, 124-125. New York: Metropolitan Museum of Art, 1987.

This version has the traditional verses and directions for a circle dance.

"Skip to My Lou." In *Singing Bee! A Collection of Favorite Children's Songs*, compiled by Jane Hart, pictures by Anita Lobel, 90-91. New York: Lothrop, Lee & Shepard, 1982.

This version has the traditional verses, including "lost my partner" and "I'll find another one," and contains directions for a circle game and dance.

KEYWORDS

Chorus — the refrain of a song, which is exactly the same each time it is sung and follows each verse.

Phrase — a division of a melody line that has been compared to a line of poetry or a sentence in prose.

Play party — a social gathering, especially of young people, characteristic of the rural United States, consisting of games performed to the singing of ballads and clapping, usually without instrumental accompaniment (*Webster's Third New International Dictionary*, 1,737)

Verse — similar to a poetic stanza; a term used for sections of a song.

EXPOSITION

1. Ask the students whether they ever play singing games at parties. Some may mention musical chairs.

2. Explain that in American pioneer times, people socialized by playing singing games. These games were called play-party games.

3. Show the cover of *Skip to My Lou* and ask whether any students have ever sung or played that song. Explain that "Skip to My Lou" is a play-party game and that *Lou* is an old word for "sweetheart" (*Go In and Out the Window*, 125).

4. Point out the music at the front of the book and sing it for the students. As you sing the four phrases, hold up a finger for the number of the phrase. Ask the students whether any of the phrases were identical (phrases one and three are the same).

5. Explain that this picture book is an adaptation of the folk song and that the words of the song have been written by Westcott to create a story.

DEVELOPMENT

1. Read the book. Sing the chorus and encourage the students to join in.

2. Have the students list the animals in the order in which they appear and sing the phrases for each animal. (Draw the animals ahead of time on posterboard so you can hold them up to prompt students for the next verse.)

3. Practice the whole song, using the animal pictures. Point out that the fourth line of each verse is "Skip to my Lou, my darling!"

RECAPITULATION

1. Ask the students how they would move to this song if they were at a play-party and were making it into a game. Does the title give any hints?

2. Divide the students into two square-dance sets of four pairs each (this is a total of sixteen students). Practice with one square at a time.

3. In each square, assign three pairs to animal parts, with the fourth pair dancing to "Skip to My Lou."

4. As the whole class sings, the corresponding animal pairs step into the circle on the first line and back out on the second. For example, they go into the circle on the words "Flies in the sugarbowl" and out on the words "Shoo fly shoo."

5. Everyone claps throughout.

6. On the chorus, everyone joins hands and skips to the left for two phrases and to the right for two phrases.

    Left: Skip, skip, skip to my Lou

            Skip, skip, skip to my Lou

    Right: Skip, skip, skip to my Lou

            Skip to my Lou, my darling

CODA

1. To teach the traditional versions of the song, consult the song collections in the "Resources" section.

2. These versions include the game that was likely played at a play party. After the students seem comfortable with the animal square-dance version, teach the play-party game.

History

The Boy Who Loved Music by David Lasker

Cowboy Dreams by Dayal Kaur Khalsa

The Erie Canal, illustrated by Peter Spier

Follow the Drinking Gourd, story and pictures by Jeanette Winter

Mozart Tonight by Julie Downing

Ragtime Tumpie by Alan Schroeder

THE BOY WHO LOVED MUSIC

By David Lasker.
Illustrated by Joe Lasker.
New York: Viking Press, 1979.

Written from the viewpoint of a horn player in Austrian Prince Esterhazy's court orchestra, this story is an account of the circumstances surrounding the composition of the *Farewell* Symphony by Franz Joseph Haydn in 1772.

Lesson grade level: 3 and up

THEME

In studying the life and music of Haydn, the composer who established the classical music forms, students will examine the structure of the symphony.

RESOURCES

Hurd, Michael. "Haydn." In *The Oxford Junior Companion to Music*, 2nd ed., 170-171. New York: Oxford University Press, 1979.

This two-page biography includes a listing of Haydn's main works.

McLeish, Kenneth, and Valerie McLeish. "Haydn." In *The Oxford First Companion to Music*, F11. New York: Oxford University Press, 1982.

This one-page biography includes the melody of the Andante movement from Haydn's *Surprise* Symphony.

Thompson, Wendy. *Joseph Haydn*. Composer's World. New York: Viking, 1991.

As the series title suggests, this biography provides much information about eighteenth-century life in the Hapsburg empire as well as examining Haydn's contribution to the classical period in music. The book includes many paintings from the time and full-size excerpts from Haydn's music.

DISCOGRAPHY

Haydn, Joseph. *Symphony no. 45* (Farewell). Derek Solomons, L'Estro Armonico. Sony Classics (Digital Masters). MDT 46507. Sound cassette.

KEYWORDS

Adagio—a tempo indication to play slowly; often the tempo marking of the second movement of a symphony.

Allegro assai—a tempo indication to play quite fast; often the tempo marking of the first and last movements of a symphony.

Andante—a tempo indication to play moderately, faster than adagio but slower than allegro.

Bass viol—the largest and lowest-sounding instrument in the viol family, which predated the violin family.

Haydn, Franz Joseph (1732-1809)—one of the main composers of the classical period; Haydn is known for developing the symphony, sonata, and string quartet forms, particularly influencing Mozart in the latter.

Horn—in the eighteenth century there were both coiled hunting horns, which could only play a fundamental tone and its harmonic series, and an orchestral horn, which had added tubing, or "crooks," to produce more notes.

Menuet (minuet)—a French dance in 3/4 meter; became the standard third movement in the symphonies of Haydn and Mozart.

Movement—a section of a larger musical work such as a symphony.

KEYWORDS—(*Continued*)

Presto—a very fast tempo; often the tempo marking for the last movement of a symphony. Presto is faster than allegro assai.

Symphony—a piece for orchestra traditionally consisting of four movements of predetermined form and different tempos; the symphony developed from the opera overture, which when played in concerts was called a *sinfonia*.

EXPOSITION

1. Sing the words "Papa Haydn's dead and gone, but his memory lingers on" to the *Surprise* Symphony melody (see *The Oxford First Companion to Music*). Explain that the composer was called "Papa Haydn" because he lived longer than most people of his time and was helpful to younger composers.

2. Give the students background information on Haydn, including his birth and death dates and the number of pieces he composed.

3. Ask whether the students know what a symphony is. Some will say it's a group of instruments, because it is often used interchangeably for the word *orchestra*. Explain that the derivation of *symphony* is "sounding together," and that the piece usually consists of four movements of contrasting tempos and forms.

4. Show the cover of *The Boy Who Loved Music* and point out the hunting horn and the grand castle in the background.

DEVELOPMENT

1. Read the introductory material and ask the students to listen during the reading of the story for the way in which musicians were treated in the eighteenth century. (This might be a good time to explain that the eighteenth century is the same as the 1700s.)

2. Read the story, leading discussions on each page. Have the students compare the life of the nobility to that of the musicians. (Thompson's biography gives some statistics on the cost of constructing Esterháza palace.)

3. Discuss the instruments that are pictured and how they differ from modern instruments. Note and explain the difference between the hunting horn and the one used in the orchestra.

4. Play a recording of the Adagio section of the last movement of the *Farewell* Symphony. Can the students tell when the instrumentalists start to leave? What instruments are left at the end? (Thompson lists the instruments in the order in which they left as follows: oboes, horns, bassoons, double basses [bass viols], then each pair of violinists, until only Haydn and Tomasini, the concertmaster, were left.)

RECAPITULATION

1. Using biographical sources on Haydn, compile a list of the types of pieces he composed and the total number of each type (for example, he wrote about 106 symphonies). Emphasize that many of the works were written on demand and that the symphonies had four movements each.

2. List the movement titles of Haydn's *Farewell* Symphony. Explain that this classical form was solidly established by Haydn.

3. Point out that the titles are tempo markings. List these markings and their definitions.

4. Investigate other symphony movements by bringing in recordings by Haydn and other classical composers such as Beethoven and Mozart. List and compare the tempo markings.

5. Use a music dictionary or encyclopedia to define unknown terms.

CODA

1. For a more in-depth investigation, listen to recordings of various symphonies. See whether the students can guess the tempo indications for the movements.

COWBOY DREAMS

By Dayal Kaur Khalsa.
New York: Clarkson N. Potter, 1990.

A little girl dreams of being a cowboy and rides a bannister horse and sings cowboy songs.

Lesson grade level: 2 and up

THEME

Students learn songs of the Old West, study paintings that portray a cowboy's life, and discover the classical piece that is used as the Lone Ranger's theme song.

RESOURCES

Charles M. Russell: Paintings of the Old American West, introduction and commentaries by Louis Chapin. New York: Crown, 1978.

Seventy-three color reproductions of Russell's paintings are included, with a facing page of description of each.

Cobblestone 3, "Frederic Remington: His Life and Art" (November 1982).

This entire issue is devoted to Remington and his paintings of the West and includes an article that compares his work to that of Charles Russell.

Freedman, Russell. *Cowboys of the Wild West*. New York: Clarion Books, 1985.

With photographs from the Library of Congress and archives from western states, Freedman presents a realistic view of a cowboy's life in the late 1800s.

Gerrard, Roy. *Rosie and the Rustlers*. New York: Farrar, Straus & Giroux, 1989.

Told in ballad form, the story relates how Rosie Jones and her ranch hands foiled Greasy Ben and his "ruffianly" men from rustling Rosie's herd.

"I'm a Poor Lonesome Cowboy." In *Cowboys and the Songs They Sang*, compiled and with text by S. J. Sackett, settings by Lionel Nowak, 46. New York: William R. Scott, 1967.

The Metropolitan Museum of Art in association with the Buffalo Bill Historical Center (comps.). *Songs of the Wild West*. Commentary by Alan Axelrod. Arrangements by Dan Fox. New York: Simon & Schuster, 1991.

In this collection of songs about the Old West, each song is accompanied by a narrative describing either the song's lyrics or the art reproductions that correspond to the song. The anthology includes "Goodbye Old Paint," "Home on the Range," and "The Cowboy's Lament" ("Streets of Laredo").

Raboff, Ernest Lloyd. *Frederic Remington*. New York: Harper & Row, 1988.

Fifteen color reproductions of Remington's works accompany the brief biography.

"Red River Valley." In *Go In and Out the Window: An Illustrated Songbook for Young People*, music arranged and edited by Dan Fox, commentary by Claude Marks, 108-109. New York: Metropolitan Museum of Art, 1987.

Rossini, Gioacchino. "William Tell Overture." In *Easy Piano Classics*, (compiled by) Philip Hawthorn, edited by Jenny Tyler and Helen Davies, music arrangements by Daniel Scott, 39. Usborne Learn to Play. Tulsa, Okla.: EDC, 1990.

This is an easy-to-play piano version of the orchestral theme.

Rounds, Glen. *Cowboys*. New York: Holiday House, 1991.

With a few sentences per page and action-filled illustrations, Rounds describes a day in the life of a cowboy.

Sharmat, Marjorie Weinman. *Gila Monsters Meet You at the Airport*. New York: Macmillan, 1980.

A New York City boy who is moving to the West is convinced that gila monsters will meet him at the airport.

DISCOGRAPHY

Copland, Aaron. "Billy the Kid—Ballet Suite." *Copland—Greatest Hits*. Eugene Ormandy, Philadelphia Orchestra. RCA Victor. BMG Music, 1991. 60837-4-RG. Sound cassette.

Rossini, Gioacchino. "William Tell Overture: Finale." *TV Classics*. Arthur Fiedler, Boston Pops. RCA Victor. BMG Music, 1992. 09026-60935-4. Sound cassette.

This overture finale has become almost inseparably associated with the cowboy character the Lone Ranger ever since it was used as the theme song for the radio and TV series.

KEYWORDS

Claves—a rhythm instrument comprising two sticks about eight to ten inches long; one stick strikes the other, which is held still.

Dotted-eighth/sixteenth note pattern—a rhythmic pattern equivalent to one beat, often used as an accompaniment figure to represent the sound of horses' hooves.

Hopalong Cassidy—the cowboy hero of a series of forty television shows that ran from June 1949 to December 1951.

The Lone Ranger—the hero of a radio show by the same name that began in 1933 and was followed by a TV version that ran from 1949-1957; also well known were his sidekick, Tonto, and horse, Silver.

Paint horse—another name for a pinto (*pinto* means "spotted" or "painted" in Spanish and refers to the white splotches on the horse's body).

EXPOSITION

1. There are two ways you can approach introducing the songs of the Wild West. One would be to dress up in cowboy gear and come in riding a hobby horse and singing "Goodbye Old Paint." The other would be to put on a recording of the opening of "The Lone Ranger" (the *William Tell* Overture). Your own personal involvement in cowboy lore will be the determinant.

2. Ask the students what they know about cowboys. Depending on the area of the country, some will have first-hand information and some will have knowledge of television cowboys.

3. Read Sharmat's *Gila Monsters Meet You at the Airport* for an example of how a boy from the West might perceive the East and vice versa.

4. Play the musical theme from "The Lone Ranger." Explain that the Lone Ranger and Hopalong Cassidy were popular radio and television characters in western shows.

DEVELOPMENT

1. Read *Cowboy Dreams*, singing the songs when the lyrics are printed.

2. Using *Songs of the Wild West, Cowboys of the Wild West*, and *Cowboys* as resources, discuss the life of a cowboy in the Old West.

3. Play the dotted-eighth/sixteenth rhythm on a keyboard, claves, or coconut-shell halves. Ask the students to tell you the first thing that comes to their minds. Hopefully they will hear the clip, clop of horses' hooves.

4. Teach the students "Goodbye Old Paint," playing the dotted rhythm on the claves as an accompaniment.

5. Because the narrator in *Cowboy Dreams* mentions going to the Metropolitan Museum of Art to look at paintings of horses, share the paintings from *Songs of the Wild West*.

RECAPITULATION

1. Teach the songs mentioned in *Cowboy Dreams* and have the students compare the information. Which depict the beauty of the Old West and which depict the realities of cowboy life?

2. Have the students find pictures of the West and horses using the books and articles on Remington and Russell.

3. Plan a readers theatre presentation of *Cowboy Dreams* using narrators, pantomime, and a chorus to sing the songs.

CODA

1. Using the facts from the songs and works of art, construct and paint a backdrop to be used for the readers theatre presentation.

2. Listen to the tapes of the old cowboy radio shows. Discuss the part music played in these shows.

3. Listen to the recording of Aaron Copland's "Billy the Kid—Ballet Suite." Have students try to identify the melodies from cowboy songs. "Goodbye Old Paint" is one of them.

4. Read *Rosie and the Rustlers* and compare the illustrations to the paintings of Remington and Russell.

THE ERIE CANAL

Illustrated by Peter Spier.
Garden City, N.Y.: Doubleday, 1970.

Spier's illustrated version of the song "Low Bridge! Everybody Down" gives a visual history of the Erie Canal, which provided a commercial link between the Atlantic Ocean and the Great Lakes in the 1800s.

Lesson grade level: 4 and up

THEME

Students discover the significance of the Erie Canal to commerce in New York State as they learn the song "Low Bridge! Everybody Down."

RESOURCES

Cobblestone 3, "The Erie Canal" (October 1982).

This entire issue of *Cobblestone* has articles on various aspects of the history of the Erie Canal.

Cohen-Straytner, Barbara, ed. *Popular Music, 1900-1919: An Annotated Guide to American Popular Songs*, 228. Detroit, Mich.: Gale Research, 1988.

This annotated guide lists "Low Bridge — Everybody Down" or "Fifteen Years on the Erie Canal" as a 1913 song written by Thomas S. Allen and now accepted as a folk song.

"The Erie Canal." In *Fireside Book of Folk Songs*, selected and edited by Margaret Bradford Boni, arranged for the piano by Norman Lloyd, illustrated by Alice Provensen and Martin Provensen, 37-39. New York: Simon & Schuster, 1947.

Besides being in a lower key, this version is slightly different melodically than the one in Spier's book. (This is the version I remember being taught.)

Macmillan, Dianne M. "I've Got an Old Mule." *Highlights for Children* (May 1984): 22-23.

Each line in the song "Low Bridge! Everybody Down" is explained with facts, figures, and definitions.

KEYWORDS

Chorus — the refrain or recurring phrase of a song.

Major key — a group of tones related to a common keynote that follows this ascending scale pattern of whole (W) and half (H) notes: WWHWWWH.

Minor key — a group of tones related to a common keynote that follows this ascending scale pattern of whole (W) and half (H) notes: WHWWHWW.

Verse — a stanza in a song; in each stanza, the words are different but the melody is the same.

EXPOSITION

1. Show the students the cover of *The Erie Canal* and tell them the reasons for constructing the Erie Canal (Spier relates these at the back of the book).

2. Show a map of New York State and trace the canal's route from Albany to Buffalo.

3. Discuss some of the terms in the book, such as *canal, barge*, and *lock*.

DEVELOPMENT

1. Go through Spier's book the first time without reading the text. Discuss each picture, asking the students to point out all the details they notice. Be sure to point out the role of the mule. What happens when barges meet going in different directions?

2. Tell the students that the words in the book are the words to a song that was written in 1913 but is considered a folk song. Read or sing the text.

3. Discuss the facts in the text, using the information at the back of the book or in the *Highlights* article.

4. Sing the song again and ask the students to tell you whether they notice any difference in the music during the verses and during the chorus.

5. Explain that the verse is in a minor key and the chorus is in a major key. The two keys are related, with the same key signature, but the sound is different.

6. Play the G-major scale (GABCDEF#G) and then the E-minor scale (EF#GABCDE). Point out that each has the same sharp note, F-sharp, but the pattern of whole steps and half steps is different. Ask whether they can determine a difference in mood.

RECAPITULATION

1. Teach the song, beginning with the chorus. As you practice the verse, point out that the first two lines have the same melody and so does the last line.

2. As a class compile a list of questions about the Erie Canal. Assign groups of students to the magazine articles and books on the Erie Canal and ask them to gather information to answer the class questions.

3. Some students could draw a map tracing the route of the Erie Canal.

4. To create a musical report on the Erie Canal, alternate singing a line of the song with a class question and answer that relates to that line.

CODA

1. As a class project, construct a model of the Erie Canal, with each student contributing a part of the diorama.

FOLLOW THE DRINKING GOURD

Story and pictures by Jeanette Winter.
New York: Alfred A. Knopf, 1988.

Peg Leg Joe uses the song "Follow the Drinking Gourd" to teach the slaves how to reach the North and freedom.

Lesson grade level: 4 and up

THEME

Students investigate the history of the Underground Railroad as they learn the mnemonic song, "Follow the Drinking Gourd."

RESOURCES

"Follow the Drinking Gourd." In *Bluegrass Greatest Hits*, adapted by Sonny Davis, 22-23. Ojai, Calif.: Creative Concepts, 1977.

This rock piano version omits some of the verses that are in Winter's book and adds a new verse.

Krupp, E. C. *The Big Dipper and You*, illustrated by Robin Rector Krupp, 19. New York: Morrow Junior Books, 1989.

This informative book discusses facts we now know about the Big Dipper and some of the lore from the past.

Levine, Ellen. *If You Traveled on the Underground Railroad*. New York: Scholastic, 1988.

Written in a question-and-answer format, this book explains the purpose of the Underground Railroad, the origin of its name, and the methods and people used to operate it.

Winter, Jeanette. *Follow the Drinking Gourd*. Hightstown, N.J.: McGraw-Hill Media/Educational Enrichment Materials, 1990. 1 filmstrip, 1 sound cassette.

This filmstrip text follows the book's text exactly. The melody of the song serves as an instrumental accompaniment to the narration; however, whenever the lyrics are printed in the story, they are sung on the filmstrip. The first verse and chorus are sung at the end of the story.

DISCOGRAPHY

"Follow the Drinking Gourd." *Songs of the Civil War*. Ritchie Havens. Columbia Records. CT-48607. Sound cassette.

"Follow the Drinking Gourd." *The Weavers: Greatest Hits*. Vanguard Recording Society. CVSD-15-16. Sound cassette.

"Inchworm." *Anne Murray Sings for the Sesame Street Generation*. CTW C-79006. Sound cassette.

KEYWORDS

Chorus—the refrain or recurring phrase of a song.

Folk song—a song originating from the people of a country or region.

Underground Railroad—a name given to the series of safe houses for runaway slaves on their way to freedom in the North; the name possibly derives from a hunting expression for a quarry that disappears into thin air and is said to be following an "underground road."

Verse—a stanza in a song; in each stanza, the words are different but the melody is the same.

EXPOSITION

1. Ask students how they memorize things. Have they ever made up a song or chant as a device for remembering?

2. Sing or play a recording of part of "Inchworm" ("two and two are four, four and four are eight, eight and eight are sixteen, sixteen and sixteen are thirty-two").

3. Another example that most children will know is "Do Re Mi" from *The Sound of Music*.

4. Discuss the terms for directions: north, south, east, west. Ask the students how they would find north in the dark. Discuss the North Star and the Big Dipper constellation.

DEVELOPMENT

1. Show the jacket cover of *Follow the Drinking Gourd*. Identify the Big Dipper. Explain what a gourd is and that hollowed gourds were used for drinking water.

2. Discuss the people in the picture and see whether the students can guess what is happening and when the story took place.

3. Read the story, singing the melody on the italicized words. If you are unsure of the song, show Winter's filmstrip.

4. After reading the story, read the author's "A Note About the Story." Discuss the Underground Railroad and the conductor, Peg Leg Joe.

5. Show the students the song on the last page and discuss the terms *chorus* and *verse*. Determine whether the song words in the story were the chorus or verses. Have the students sing the chorus.

RECAPITULATION

1. Using maps or atlases of the United States, have the students find the Tombigbee, Tennessee, and Ohio rivers mentioned in the author's note.

2. Using the book *If You Traveled on the Underground Railroad*, discuss the various ways the slaves escaped to freedom.

3. Teach the song "Follow the Drinking Gourd," emphasizing the various route clues in each verse. Refer to the illustrations to show how Peg Leg Joe marked the route.

4. As a class, write a poem with the title, "If You Traveled on the Underground Railroad." Each student adds a line with a fact learned from Winter's or Levine's book.

CODA

1. Assign projects to groups of students. Possible projects could be reports on the Underground Railroad, a play using the song "Follow the Drinking Gourd," or maps outlining the Underground Railroad route.

2. Investigate other "conductors" on the Underground Railroad such as Harriet Tubman.

MOZART TONIGHT

By Julie Downing.
New York: Bradbury Press, 1991.

Based on Mozart's letters and accounts of the day, *Mozart Tonight* is a fictionalized story of Mozart's life, from his days as a prodigy to the performance of his opera *Don Giovanni*.

Lesson grade level: 3 and up

THEME

Students will investigate the life and times of the musical genius Mozart.

RESOURCES

Brighton, Catherine. *Mozart: Scenes from the Childhood of the Great Composer*. New York: Doubleday, 1990.

Writing from the viewpoint of Mozart's sister, Nannerl, Brighton describes the duo's recital tours through Paris, London, Chelsea (it was not then part of London), and Vienna, ending as Mozart embarks on a solo tour through Italy.

Crespi, Francesca. *The Magic Flute: The Story of Mozart's Opera*. Retold by Margaret Greaves. New York: Henry Holt, 1989.

The story line from *The Magic Flute* is told in picture-book format.

Fradin, Dennis Brindell. "Wolfgang Amadeus Mozart." In *Remarkable Children: Twenty Who Made History*, 3-12. Boston: Little, Brown, 1987.

Concentrating on Mozart's years as a prodigy touring Europe, Fradin supplies anecdotes of Mozart's precocity and describes the rigors of his musical career.

Hurd, Michael. "Mozart." In *The Oxford Junior Companion to Music*, 2nd ed., 234-235. New York: Oxford University Press, 1979.

This article succinctly describes Mozart's life and music and includes a list of his main works.

Tames, Richard. *Wolfgang Amadeus Mozart*. New York: Franklin Watts, 1991.

This thirty-two page biography explores Mozart's life from birth to death, with many paintings and reproductions from the time period, a bibliography, time line, and glossary.

Thompson, Wendy. *Wolfgang Amadeus Mozart*. Composer's World. New York: Viking Press, 1990.

This detailed biography includes paintings of the period and many full-page musical excerpts.

KEYWORDS

Clavichord—a keyboard instrument popular in the sixteenth through eighteenth centuries that was shaped like a rectangular box and used primarily in homes because of its soft sound; a forerunner of the piano.

Mozart, Wolfgang Amadeus (1756-1791)—one of the main composers of the classical period; Mozart's genius is evident in all the classical forms.

Opera—a play in which the characters sing, rather than speak, the parts.

Overture—a piece of instrumental music that serves as an introduction to a longer musical or dramatic work such as an opera or play.

Pianoforte—an older name for the piano; the name signifies that the instrument can play softly (piano) or loudly (forte) depending on the touch of the player.

Prodigy—a highly gifted and talented child.

Sonata—a form of instrumental music prevalent from the mid-eighteenth century on.

Symphony—a musical composition for orchestra, usually divided into four movements.

EXPOSITION

1. Ask the students what they know about Mozart. (Be sure to emphasize the correct pronunciation of his name: Moh-tsart.) Briefly discuss the time period in which he lived and his birth and death dates.

2. Tell the students that Mozart was a musical prodigy and explain the term. If possible, play a piece that he wrote when he was young, such as the Minuet in F, which he composed at the age of six (see Thompson's biography for the music).

3. Relate that Mozart wrote a number of famous operas. Discuss the form of an opera and how it differs from a play.

4. Discuss the cover picture and determine that the keyboard is a pianoforte. Explain what the term means and that the ability to produce sound both softly and loudly on a keyboard was not present in the earlier keyboard instruments such as the harpsichord and the clavichord.

5. Read the introduction to Downing's book.

DEVELOPMENT

1. As you read the story, encourage the students to ask questions or comment on the illustrations, which offer much information about life in the eighteenth century. In particular, point out the various instruments depicted.

2. Using a time line and a map of Europe, trace the events in Mozart's life. Consult Brighton's book for more information on Mozart's tours through Europe. Thompson's biography has a map with the tours marked.

3. Ask the students to compare the life of a musician and composer of today with that of an eighteenth-century musician. How are modern musicians treated? Obviously there aren't court musicians today. Do our musicians get paid by the government?

4. Ask the students whether they think Mozart's music was affected by the events of his life. What does Downing's story suggest?

5. Discuss the musical forms mentioned in the book: sonata, overture, and opera. Show the students Crespi's book on *The Magic Flute* and briefly describe the plot.

RECAPITULATION

1. As a class, plan a presentation on Mozart, possibly to coincide with his birthday, January 27. Use the picture books and biographies listed as resource materials.

2. Have groups of students gather information on Mozart and the eighteenth century. Assign topics such as Early Life, Family, Later Life, Operas, Eighteenth-Century Austria, Tours as a Child, Prodigies.

3. Encourage the students to add music to their presentations as examples of his work or as a background to an oral report.

4. Allow some students to use their artistic strengths in painting a backdrop that features the clothing and decorations in the illustrations in Downing's book.

CODA

1. Read Crespi's *The Magic Flute*. Investigate this opera with the students. The wealth of fascinating characters and the similarity to fantasy literature will make this introduction to opera relatively easy.

RAGTIME TUMPIE

By Alan Schroeder.
Paintings by Bernie Fuchs.
Boston: Little, Brown, 1989.

In this fictionalized account of the early childhood of ragtime dancer Josephine Baker, Tumpie (as young Josephine was called) can't stop dancing to lively ragtime music.

Lesson grade level: 3 and up

THEME

After hearing the ragtime music of Scott Joplin and the story of Josephine Baker growing up in St. Louis, students will experiment with ragtime's syncopation.

RESOURCES

Blesh, Rudi. *Classic Piano Rags: Complete Original Music for 81 Rags*. New York: Dover, 1973.

Along with the original music and sheet music covers, Blesh provides background information on the era and many of the ragtime composers.

Blesh, Rudi, and Harriet Janis. *They All Played Ragtime*. New York: Oak, 1971.

Complete with photographs and musical excerpts, this history of ragtime is both exhaustive and entertaining.

Chronicle of America. 525. Mount Kisco, N.Y.: Chronicle, n.d.

This chronological, historical, and social account of America's history as told in newspaper format cites the publishing of Joplin's "Maple Leaf Rag."

Lieser, Julia F. "Ragtime and Scott Joplin." *Cobblestone* 4 (October 1983): 12-14.

This article gives a brief history of ragtime music and the part Joplin played in its promotion and success.

Mitchell, Barbara. *Raggin': A Story About Scott Joplin*. A Carolrhoda Creative Minds Book. Minneapolis, Minn.: Carolrhoda Books, 1987.

In this fictionalized, fifty-five-page biography, Mitchell describes Joplin's musical career while presenting an account of the everyday life of southern blacks after the Civil War.

Preston, Katherine. *Scott Joplin*. Black Americans of Achievement. New York: Chelsea House, 1988.

Preston provides a detailed biography of Joplin, including much information on the cities and lifestyles of the time. Many photographs of Joplin and his acquaintances and his sheet music covers are included.

DISCOGRAPHY

Joplin, Scott. *Scott Joplin: Greatest Hits*. Dick Hyman, James Levine, piano. RCA Victor. BMG Music, 1991. 60842-4-RG. Sound cassette.

Joplin, Scott. *Scott Joplin: The Red Back Book*. The New England Conservatory Ragtime Ensemble, Gunther Schuller. Angel S-36060. Sound recording.

The Sting. Marvin Hamlisch. MCA Records. MCA-1625. Sound cassette.

KEYWORDS

Accent—emphasis or stress on a note or chord, usually on the first beat of a measure.

Ragtime music—American music popular during the 1890s and early 1900s that featured syncopated rhythms and was written and performed primarily by African Americans.

Syncopation—an uneven rhythm caused by moving the accent in a measure of music from a strong beat to a weaker one. This shift can be accomplished by resting or not playing on the first beat of a measure.

EXPOSITION

1. Play a recording of ragtime music, asking students to clap on the beat. The bass part will have notes on the beat, but the melody will be syncopated, or off the beat. Explain that this is ragtime music, or music that is ragged, or uneven. Compare it to a torn cloth or hem.

2. Demonstrate syncopation by having one person clap for each syllable in the word *syncopation* while you clap in between the beats on the offbeats (see example 1, below). Next try a pattern that has a rest on the first beat (see example 2, below). Have the students clap on the beat. Next, shift the accent to the offbeat (see example 3, below).

    1. clap   clap   clap   clap
             syn   co   pa   tion

    2. clap   clap   clap   clap
             rag-ge-   dy mu-   sic

    3. clap   clap   clap   clap
        rag-gin   a hot   tune

3. Clap each pattern with the words and have the students repeat them until they can do all of them in succession.

4. Relate the time period of ragtime's popularity and explain that ragtime music was replaced by jazz. Ask students whether they know the movie *The Sting*. This 1974 movie brought about a popular revival of ragtime music by featuring the music of Scott Joplin.

5. Explain that *Ragtime Tumpie* is a fiction book but emphasize that the author based the story on the early life of a famous black dancer, Josephine Baker. She grew up in St. Louis, Missouri, a center of ragtime music. Ask the students to pay attention during the reading of the book to the information about the music and the lifestyles of the characters.

DEVELOPMENT

1. Read *Ragtime Tumpie* to the students, allowing plenty of time for them to absorb the flavor of the illustrations and glean information about that period of American history.

2. Discuss all aspects of the time and setting mentioned in the story: for example, the Rosebud Cafe (owned by another ragtime composer, Tom Turpin), barrel houses, riverboats, and the Booker T. Washington Theater. (Supplement the discussions with information from *Chronicle of America, They All Played Ragtime*, or one of Joplin's biographies.)

3. Have the students list and discuss all the musical terms and instruments mentioned in the book. (Unknown terms can be assigned for further investigation.)

RECAPITULATION

1. Play the same or another ragtime selection and ask the students to imagine the musicians and dancers.

2. As a whole group activity, encourage students to devise their own syncopated word patterns using words from *Ragtime Tumpie* or words descriptive of the time or music. In order to hear the syncopation, one group should clap a steady beat. These phrases could be put together to form a syncopated rap outlining the ragtime era.

3. As a read-aloud or as a group reading assignment, read *Raggin'* or *Scott Joplin*. Construct a time line with names, dates, and places significant to the history of ragtime. The *Chronicle of America*, arranged chronologically in a newspaper format, provides information on diverse aspects of American life.

CODA

1. Study the sheet music covers in *Classic Piano Rags* for information on cities, publishers, and lifestyles. Point out the similarity between the title page layout of *Ragtime Tumpie* and the sheet music covers. Compare the various lettering patterns. Have the students design their own sheet music covers either in the style of the ragtime era or in current style.

2. The covers also vividly portray how African Americans were perceived at the time. This visual representation along with the Joplin biographies can lead to a discussion of what life was like for African Americans at that time.

3. Ask for volunteer musicians to perform a ragtime piece. There are numerous arrangements of Joplin's "Maple Leaf Rag" and "The Entertainer" for beginning musicians.

SONG COLLECTIONS

Aaron, Tossi (comp.). *Punchinella 47: Twenty Traditional American Play Parties for Singing, Dancing, and Playing Orff Instruments.* Arranged by Tossi Aaron. Philadelphia, Pa.: Coda, 1983.

Amery, Heather (comp.). *The Usborne Children's Songbook.* Illustrated by Stephen Cartwright. Music arrangements by Barrie Carson Turner. London: Usborne, 1988.

Bley, Edgar S. (comp.). *The Best Singing Games for Children of All Ages.* New York: Sterling, 1976.

Boni, Margaret Bradford (ed. and comp.). *Fireside Book of Favorite American Songs.* Arranged by Norman Lloyd. Illustrated by Aurelius Battaglia. New York: Simon & Schuster, 1952.

_____. *Fireside Book of Folk Songs.* Arranged for the piano by Norman Lloyd. Illustrated by Alice Provensen and Martin Provensen. New York: Simon & Schuster, 1947.

Cassidy, Nancy, and John Cassidy. *The Book of Kids Songs: A Holler-Along Handbook.* Illustrated by Jim M'Guinness. Music produced by Ken Whiteley. Palo Alto, Calif.: Klutz Press, 1986.

Fox, Dan (ed.). *Go In and Out the Window: An Illustrated Songbook for Young People.* Music arranged by Dan Fox. Commentary by Claude Marks. New York: Metropolitan Museum of Art, 1987.

Glazer, Tom (comp.). *Mother Goose Songbook.* Illustrated by David McPhail. New York: Doubleday, 1990.

Hart, Jane (comp.). *Singing Bee! A Collection of Favorite Children's Songs.* Pictures by Anita Lobel. New York: Lothrop, Lee & Shepard Books, 1982.

Langstaff, Nancy, and John Langstaff (comps.). *Jim Along, Josie: A Collection of Folk Songs and Singing Games for Young Children.* Illustrated by Jan Pienkowski. New York: Harcourt Brace Jovanovich, 1970.

Mattox, Cheryl Warren (comp.). *Shake It to the One That You Love the Best: Play Songs and Lullabies from Black Musical Traditions.* Adapted by Cheryl Warren Mattox. With illustrations from the works of Varnette P. Honeywood and Brenda Joysmith. El Sobrante, Calif.: Warren-Mattox Productions, 1989.

McRae, Shirley W. (comp.). *Angel at the Door: Southern Folksongs.* St. Louis, Mo.: Magnamusic-Baton, 1981.

The Metropolitan Museum of Art in association with the Buffalo Bill Historical Center (comps.). *Songs of the Wild West.* Commentary by Alan Axelrod. Arrangements by Dan Fox. New York: Simon & Schuster, 1991.

National Gallery of Art (comp.). *An Illustrated Treasury of Songs.* Milwaukee, Wis.: Hal Leonard; New York: Rizzoli, 1991.

Seeger, Ruth Crawford (comp.). *American Folk Songs for Children, in Home, School, and Nursery School: A Book for Children, Parents, and Teachers*. Illustrated by Barbara Cooney. New York: Doubleday, 1948.

Wessells, Katharine Tyler (comp.). *The Golden Song Book*. Music arranged by Katharine Tyler Wessells. Illustrated by Kathy Allert. New York: Golden Press, 1981.

Winn, Marie (ed. and comp.). *The Fireside Book of Children's Songs*. Musical arrangements by Allan Miller. Illustrations by John Alcorn. New York: Simon & Schuster, 1966.

_____. *The Fireside Book of Fun and Games Songs*. Musical arrangements by Allan Miller. Illustrations by Whitney Darrow, Jr. New York: Simon & Schuster, 1974.

Yolen, Jane (ed.). *The Lullaby Songbook*. With musical arrangements by Adam Stemple. Pictures by Charles Mikolaycak. San Diego, Calif.: Harcourt Brace Jovanovich, 1986.

_____. *Rounds About Rounds*. Musical arrangements by Barbara Green. Illustrations by Gail Gibbons. New York: Franklin Watts, 1977.

ANNOTATED BIBLIOGRAPHY SUPPLEMENT

RHYTHM

Chicka Chicka Boom Boom

Fitzgerald, Ella. *Ella Fitzgerald.* Verve Music Group, 2000. CD.
  This compilation of recordings of Ella Fitzgerald evolved from the Ken Burns *Jazz* series. "Flying Home" is an example of Fitzgerald's scat singing. "Let's Call the Whole Thing Off" is a duet with Louis Armstrong.

Orgill, Roxane. *If I Only Had a Horn: Young Louis Armstrong.* Illustrated by Leonard Jenkins. Boston: Houghton Mifflin, 1997.
  Basing her story on information from Armstrong's autobiographies and other sources, Orgill tells the story of Louis Armstrong's first experiences with music and how he got his first cornet.

Tate, Eleanora E. *African American Musicians.* New York: John Wiley & Sons, 2000.
  African American Musicians contains short biographies in chronological order from Elizabeth Taylor Greenfield, a singer in the mid-1800s to Queen Latifah, a rap star of the 1990s. Biographies of Louis Armstrong and Ella Fitzgerald are included.

Completed Hickory Dickory Dock

"Here We Go Round the Mulberry Bush." Pete Seeger. In *American Folk, Game & Activity Songs for Children.* Smithsonian Folkways Recordings, 2000. SFW CD 45056. CD.

Knock at a Star: A Child's Introduction to Poetry. Rev. ed. [Compiled by] X. J. Kennedy and Dorothy M. Kennedy. Illustrated by Karen Lee Baker. Boston: Little, Brown, 1999.
  This anthology includes a wide variety of poems divided into four sections: "What Do Poems Do?" "What's Inside a Poem?" "Special Kinds of Poetry," and "Do It Yourself." Explanations and suggestions for activities are included.
  Coda: The section on limericks states that "the rhythm gallops."

Crocodile Beat

Fleming, Denise. *Barnyard Banter.* New York: Henry Holt, 1994.
  Each two-page spread introduces a farm animal, its location, and its sound. For example, "cows in the pasture, moo, moo, moo" and "roosters in the barnyard, cock-a-doodle-doo."
  Coda: Each two-page spread has four beats with a combination of eighth-note and quarter-note rhythms.

Fleming, Denise. *In the Small, Small Pond.* New York: Henry Holt, 1993.
  Using action-packed rhymes, such as, "waddle, wade, geese parade" and "wiggle, jiggle, tadpoles wriggle," Fleming describes the animals in the pond throughout spring until snow heralds winter's coming.
  Coda: Each two-page spread has four beats with a combination of eighth-note and quarter-note rhythms. The one exception is the triplet beat of "whirligig."

Miss Mary Mack: And Other Children's Street Rhymes

Hoberman, Mary Ann. *Miss Mary Mack: A Hand-Clapping Rhyme.* Illustrated by Nadine Bernard Westcott. Boston: Little, Brown, 1998.

 In this picture book Hoberman has added verses to the traditional song to create a story about Miss Mary Mack and the elephant. The music is included along with a hand-clapping game.

 Recapitulation: Use this book to teach the song.

"Mary Mack." Ella Jenkins. In *Smithsonian Folkways Children's Music Collection.* Smithsonian Folkways Recordings, 1998. SF CD 45043. CD.

"Miss Mary Mack." In *Brown Girl in the Ring: An Anthology of Song Games from the Eastern Caribbean,* collected and documented by Alan Lomax, J. D. Elder, and Bess Lomax Hawes, 36. New York: Pantheon Books, 1997.

 Recapitulation: This version from Trinidad has a slightly different melody. The accompanying notes include the clapping pattern used by the Trinidadian children.

One, Two, Skip a Few! First Number Rhymes. Illustrated by Roberta Arenson. Brooklyn, N.Y.: Barefoot Books, 1998.

 This collection of number rhymes includes favorites such as "One Potato," and "There Were Ten in the Bed."

Possum Come A-Knockin'

Fleischman, Paul. "The Quiet Evenings Here." In *Big Talk: Poems for Four Voices*, illustrated by Beppe Giacobbe, 8. Cambridge, Mass.: Candlewick Press, 2000.

 Fleischman has expanded the two voices of *Joyful Noise* with three poems for four voices. The parts are color-coded and arranged as if on a musical staff.

 Recapitulation: This rhythmic four-voice poem fits nicely with *Possum Come A-Knockin'* because it includes similar characters and actions, for example, "grandma rockin'," "brother whittlin'," "sister hummin'," and "grandpa strummin'."

"How Possum Got His Skinny Tail." In *In a Circle Long Ago: A Treasury of Native Lore from North America,* by Nancy Van Laan, illustrated by Lisa Desimini, 88-93. New York: Apple Soup Books, 1995.

Train Song

"Casey Jones." In *Gonna Sing My Head Off! American Folk Songs for Children,* collected and arranged by Kathleen Krull, illustrated by Allen Garns, 11-13. New York: Alfred A. Knopf, 1995.

"John Henry." In *Gonna Sing My Head Off! American Folk Songs for Children,* 67-68.

Lewis, Kevin. *Chugga-Chugga Choo-Choo.* Pictures by Daniel Kirk. New York: Hyperion Books for Children, 1999.

 Using bright, bold illustrations of a toy train set, this rhythmic, rhyming picture book relates the journey of the toy train through the tracks in a young boy's room. The lines are in a 4/4 meter and include the "chugga-chugga choo-choo" and "whooooo whooooo" refrains.

 Coda: Use as another example of combinations of rhythmic values in 4/4 meter.

McCord, David. "Song of the Train." In *Noisy Poems,* collected by Jill Bennett, illustrated by Nick Sharratt, [n.p.] New York: Oxford University Press, 1996.

Suen, Anastasia. *Window Music.* Illustrated by Wade Zahares. New York: Puffin Books, 1998.
   As a mother and daughter leave grandparents and travel back to the city, they see a variety of "window music," or passing scenery. The rhyming text keeps a steady rhythm.
   Coda: Use as another example of combinations of rhythmic values in 4/4 meter. Add this to the discussion of viewpoint, that is, "window music" scenery as opposed to people viewing the train going by.

Voake, Charlotte. *Here Comes the Train.* Cambridge, Mass.: Candlewick Press, 1998.
   A father and his children ride their bikes to the footbridge to wait for the trains. As the train comes and goes, the sound increases and diminishes.
   Coda: Use this book to add the musical concepts of crescendo and diminuendo.

MELODY

All the Pretty Horses

"All the Pretty Horses." In *Lullabies: An Illustrated Songbook,* music arranged by Richard Kapp, 15-16. New York: The Metropolitan Museum of Art, 1997.

All the Pretty Little Horses: A Traditional Lullaby. Illustrated by Linda Saport. New York: Clarion Books, 1999.
   Illustrated in pastels and featuring African-Americans, this rendition of the well-known lullaby adds a second verse about a baby lamb. The music is included.

"By'm Bye." In *Lullabies: An Illustrated Songbook*, 53.

Lullabies: An Illustrated Songbook. Music arranged by Richard Kapp. New York: The Metropolitan Museum of Art; San Diego: Gulliver Books, 1997.
   Recapitulation: Use "Armenian Lullaby" and "Raisins and Almonds" as examples of lullabies in a minor key. ("Raisins and Almonds" includes the raised 7th of the harmonic minor scale.)

Fiddle-I-Fee: A Farmyard Song for the Very Young

"Barnyard Song, or, I Had a Cat." In *Gonna Sing My Head Off! American Folk Songs for Children,* collected and arranged by Kathleen Krull, illustrated by Allen Garns, 6-7. New York: Alfred A. Knopf, 1995.

"Bought Me a Cat." Pete Seeger. In *American Folk, Game & Activity Songs for Children.* Smithsonian Folkways Recordings, 2000. SFW CD 45056. CD.
   Seeger adds a few verses that are not in *Fiddle-I-Fee.* Instead of exact pitches, he imitates actual animal sounds.

Morley, Carol. *Farmyard Song.* New York: Simon & Schuster Books for Young Readers, 1995.
   This picture book version of "I Had a Cat" includes all the words, but not the music.

Georgia Music

Ahlberg, Allan. *Mockingbird*. Illustrated by Paul Howard. Cambridge, Mass.: Candlewick Press, 1998.
   This version of "Hush, Little Baby," set in the 19th century, describes a baby's birthday and the presents received from the family.
   Coda: Use this and the following picture-book version of "Hush, Little Baby" to teach the song.

Fleming, Candace. *When Agnes Caws*. Illustrated by Giselle Potter. New York: Atheneum Books for Young Readers, 1999.
   "Agnes Peregrine, daughter of a well-known ornithologist" can imitate any bird song. In searching for the pink-headed duck, she unwittingly leads a poacher to the bird and must use her talents to save the duck.
   Coda: Use this book to reinforce the rhythmic and melodic variations in bird songs.

Frazee, Marla. *Hush, Little Baby: A Folk Song with Pictures*. San Diego: Harcourt, 1999.
   In this version set in the hills of West Virginia during the 19th century, a baby will not stop crying, and the family tries to appease it with various gifts. The music and words to the traditional song are included.

Grandma's Band

"The Crawdad Song." In *Gonna Sing My Head Off! American Folk Songs for Children*, collected and arranged by Kathleen Krull, illustrated by Allen Garns, 24-25. New York: Alfred A. Knopf, 1995.

"On Top of Old Smoky." In *Gonna Sing My Head Off! American Folk Songs for Children*, collected and arranged by Kathleen Krull, illustrated by Allen Garns, 83-84. New York: Alfred A. Knopf, 1995.

"She'll Be Coming Round the Mountain." In *Gonna Sing My Head Off! American Folk Songs for Children*, collected and arranged by Kathleen Krull, illustrated by Allen Garns, 94-95. New York: Alfred A. Knopf, 1995.

Mary Wore Her Red Dress, and Henry Wore His Green Sneakers

Garcia, Jerry, and David Grisman. *What Will You Wear, Jenny Jenkins?* Song arranged and performed by Jerry Garcia and David Grisman. Illustrated by Bruce Whatley. New York: HarperCollins, 2000.
   Different color verses are added to the original song, and the illustrator adds a story that ends with the bear, Jenny Jenkins, rolling on a ball as a tightrope walker in a circus. A tape of the song performed by Garcia and Grisman is included.
   Coda: As students listen to the tape, point out that Garcia and Grisman perform the song as a duet with one asking the questions and one answering them.

Sing, Pierrot, Sing: A Picture Book in Mime

"Au Clair de la Lune." Wendy Wiseman. In *Sleepy Time Rock-A-Byes*, arranged and produced by Sari Dajani. Kidzup Productions, 1996. CD.

"Here We Go Round the Mulberry Bush." Pete Seeger. In *American Folk, Game & Activity Songs for Children*. Smithsonian Folkways Recordings, 2000. SFW CD 45056. CD.

Ten Bears in My Bed: A Goodnight Countdown

Peek, Merle. *Roll Over! A Counting Song.* Illustrated by Merle Peek. New York: Clarion Books, 1981; Reader: Jane Staab, Music: Michael Moss, Soundscape Charlesberry Productions. Houghton Mifflin, 1999.
    On the tape, *Roll Over* is read on Side A and sung on Side B.

There's a Hole in the Bucket

Ormerod, Jan. *Ms. MacDonald Has a Class.* New York: Clarion Books, 1996.
    Using the same format as the song, "Old MacDonald Had a Farm," Ormerod's Ms. MacDonald takes her class on a field trip to a farm, and from this experience they plan a presentation for parents. They practice songs, "with a tra-la here and a tra-la there," and they make costumes "with a snip snip here and a stitch stitch there," etc.
    Recapitulation: The melody line of the song is printed on most of the pages. Have the students point out the "home tone" or G in the music. Assign groups to each verse and have them perform the book with pantomimes.

Schubert, Ingrid, and Dieter Schubert. *There's a Hole in My Bucket.* Asheville, N.C.: Front Street/Lemniscaat, 1998.
    This retelling of the German folksong relates in story form the misadventures of Bear and Hedgehog as they try to repair the bucket so they can water Bear's flowers.
    Coda: Read this story and ask the students to compare this version with Westcott's.

FORM & STYLE

Bonjour, Mr. Satie

Laden, Nina. *When Pigasso Met Mootisse.* San Francisco: Chronicle Books, 1998.
    Based on the true rivalry between Picasso and Matisse, this spoof contains the characters, Pigasso, a pig who paints "in a most unusual way," and Mootisse, a bull who paints "big, bold, bright pictures." The illustrations are in the styles of the artists and contain pig and bull copies of many of the artists' famous paintings. A brief biography of both artists is at the end of the book.
    Recapitulation: Read Laden's book to emphasize the difference in the two artists' styles. After the students have looked at examples of the actual paintings, ask them to identify the derivations in the book.

Le Tord, Bijou. *A Bird or Two: A Story about Henri Matisse.* Grand Rapids, Mich.: Eerdmans Books for Young Readers, 1999.
    With illustrations that copy many of Matisse's paintings, Le Tord with simple descriptive words portrays the time Matisse spent in Nice, France, and the influence it had on his paintings.

Lowery, Linda. *Pablo Picasso.* Illustrations by Janice Lee Porter. Minneapolis: Carolrhoda Books, 1999.
    This short biography discusses Picasso's entire life, emphasizing his various painting styles, including cubism. The author recounts Picasso's friendship with cubist painter, Georges Braque, and the story behind his *Guernica* painting.

The Complete Story of the Three Blind Mice

Goodhart, Pippa. *Row, Row, Row Your Boat.* Illustrated by Stephen Lambert. New York: Crown, 1997.
Verses are added to the song to relate two children's adventures after rowing to a jungle island where they encounter different animals. The music is included.
Recapitulation: Teach as another example of a round.

MacDonald, Margaret Read, and Winifred Jaeger. *The Round Book: Rounds Kids Love to Sing.* Illustrated by Yvonne LeBrun Davis. North Haven, Conn.: Linnet Books, 1999.
This collection of 80 rounds includes a brief history of the round and suggestions for teaching them.

Trapani, Iaz. *Row Row Row Your Boat.* Dallas, Tex.: Whispering Coyote Press, 1999.
As a family of bears rows "gently down the stream," they encounter many adventures, adding new verses to the familiar song. The music is included.
Recapitulation: Teach as another example of a round.

Joyful Noise: Poems for Two Voices

Fleischman, Paul. *Big Talk: Poems for Four Voices.* Illustrated by Beppe Giacobbe. Cambridge, Mass.: Candlewick Press, 2000.
Fleischman has expanded the two voices of *Joyful Noise* with three poems for four voices. The parts are color-coded and arranged as if on a musical staff.
Coda: Introduce the term *quartet* and, following Fleischman's "helpful hints," have the students add these poems to their duet program.

Florian, Douglas. *Insectlopedia.* San Diego: Harcourt, 1998.
These insect poems are clever wordplays, but also contain factual information about the insect. They are short enough to be memorized easily.
Recapitulation: Include these poems in a presentation of insect poems.

Millen, C. M. *A Symphony for the Sheep.* Illustrated by Mary Azarian. Boston: Houghton Mifflin, 1996.
This story poem describes the process of shearing, spinning, weaving, and knitting wool to obtain a sweater. Each action has a "refrain … which was written to represent the melody of the action being described."
Recapitulation: The author includes instruction for performing the refrains as a round to make four-part harmony.

Mama Don't Allow

"Louis Armstrong." In *Great African Americans in Jazz,* Carlotta Hacker, 4-9. New York: Crabtree Publishing, 1997.
Hacker discusses Armstrong's beginnings in New Orleans and his scat singing.

"Mama Don't Allow." In *Gonna Sing My Head Off! American Folk Songs for Children,* collected and arranged by Kathleen Krull, illustrated by Allen Garns, 71-72. New York: Alfred A. Knopf, 1995.

Orgill, Roxane. *If I Only Had a Horn: Young Louis Armstrong*. Illustrated by Leonard Jenkins. Boston: Houghton Mifflin, 1997.

Basing her story on information from Armstrong's autobiographies and other sources, Orgill tells the story of Louis Armstrong's first experiences with music and how he got his first cornet.

Sabbeth, Alex. *Rubber-Band Banjos and a Java Jive Bass: Projects & Activities on the Science of Music & Sound*. Project illustrations by Laurel Aiello. New York: John Wiley & Sons, 1997.

After a chapter on sound and hearing, Sabbeth provides instructions on making stringed, wind, and percussion instruments. Explanations and background on the actual instruments are given first.

Recapitulation: Use this book for ideas on making instruments from everyday objects.

Tate, Eleanora E. *African American Musicians*. New York: John Wiley & Sons, 2000.

African American Musicians contains short biographies in chronological order from Elizabeth Taylor Greenfield, a singer in the mid-1800s to Queen Latifah, a rap star of the 1990s. Biographies of Louis Armstrong and Ella Fitzgerald are included.

Nathaniel Talking

Millen, C. M. *The Low-Down Laundry Line Blues*. Illustrated by Christine Davenier. Boston: Houghton Mifflin, 1999.

One sister has the blues, and the other tries to cheer her up. Written in rhyme, the blues section fits the pattern of the musical blues. The upbeat sister speaks in shorter be-bop style, and the laundry line is eventually used for a jump rope.

Recapitulation: Have two students or two groups take the parts of the sisters, varying the tempo according to whether it's blues or be-bop.

Tate, Eleanora E. *African American Musicians*. New York: John Wiley & Sons, 2000.

African American Musicians contains short biographies in chronological order from Elizabeth Taylor Greenfield, a singer in the mid-1800s to Queen Latifah, a rap star of the 1990s.

Coda: Biographies of W. C. Handy, "Ma" Rainey, and Bessie Smith are included.

Rondo in C

Fleming, Candace. *Gabriella's Song*. Illustrated by Giselle Potter. New York: Atheneum Books for Young Readers, 1997.

In Venice, Italy, Gabriella hears music in the melody of street vendors' songs, in the rhythm of the boats, and the harmony of flapping laundry, pigeon wings, and church bells. Her song is heard and passed on through the people in the city until a struggling composer hears it and incorporates it into his new symphony.

Development: Each of the people who hear Gabriella's song interprets it in a different way. Share this story as another example of the feelings music evokes.

Levine, Robert. *The Story of the Orchestra: Listen While You Learn about the Instruments, the Music and the Composers Who Wrote the Music!* Illustrated by Meredith Hamilton. New York: Black Dog & Leventhal, 2001.

Each period of music, its composers, and the sections of the orchestra are explained in one- or two-page entries with numerous boxes of anecdotal material. The accompanying CD provides musical excerpts that feature the composer or instrument.

Development: Play the excerpts from *Carnival of the Animals*, *The Sorcerer's Apprentice,* and *The Nutcracker* as examples of music that tells a story. The CD also contains excerpts from two of Beethoven's symphonies.

INSTRUMENTS

All Join In

Hubbell, Patricia. *Pots and Pans.* Pictures by Diane de Groat. New York: Harper Festival, 1998.
In this rhythmic, rhyming story, the baby is in the kitchen with the pots and pans. "Ching," "cling," "clang," "clink," etc., are some of the words used to describe the sounds.
Coda: Continue the investigation of the relationship between vowel sounds and pitch with this book and the poems in the following collection.

Poems Go Clang! A Collection of Noisy Verse. Illustrated by Debi Gliori. Cambridge, Mass.: Candlewick Press, 1997.
Beginning with the poem, "On the Ning Nang Nong," this collection of poems also celebrates sound in "Kitchen Sing-Song" and "Our Washing Machine." "Steel Band Jump Up" uses the words "ping pong" in imitation of a steel drum.

Berlioz the Bear

Apelt, Kathi. *Bats on Parade.* Illustrated by Melissa Sweet. New York: Morrow Junior Books, 1999.
The multiplication table is taught as the bat band marches in four sets of four clarinets up to ten sets of ten sousaphones.
Development: Use this book to emphasize the band instruments, including the wind, brass, and percussion sections.

Lithgow, John. *The Remarkable Farkle McBride.* Illustrated by C. F. Payne. New York: Simon & Schuster Books for Young Readers, 2000.
The prodigy, Farkle McBride, plays an instrument from each section of the orchestra before he decides that conducting is the best instrument for him.
Development or Coda: The illustrations realistically show the various sections of the orchestra, and a double foldout section displays the entire orchestra.

Martin, Jr., Bill. *The Maestro Plays.* Pictures by Vladimir Radunsky. New York: Henry Holt, 1994.
The "maestro" plays various instruments, and the music is described using various adverbs.
Development: Discuss with students what sounds these words would make on an instrument. Bring in various instruments and demonstrate "dizzily," "skippingly," and the other adverbs.

City Sounds

Long, Melinda. *When Papa Snores.* Pictures by Holly Meade. New York: Simon & Schuster, 2000.
A little girl cannot sleep because Papa and Nana snore. Each snore is described with a different word sound ("honnkk shooooo honnkk shooooo"), as are the household items that move in the draft (window blinds—"clinka-linka"). The items that move are repeated in a cumulative pattern.
Coda: Assign students one of the recurring lines to produce a readers' theater. A chorus can produce the sounds of the household items.

Pinkney, Brian. *Max Found Two Sticks*. New York: Aladdin Paperbacks, 1997.
Max imitates the sounds in his city block as he uses two heavy twigs to tap out rhythms on his thighs, a bucket, hatboxes, bottles, and garbage can lids.

Good Times on Grandfather Mountain

Pinkney, Brian. *Max Found Two Sticks*. New York: Aladdin Paperbacks, 1997.
Max imitates the sounds in his city block as he uses two heavy twigs to tap out rhythms on his thighs, a bucket, hatboxes, bottles, and garbage can lids.
Coda: Use with or in place of *Ty's One-Man Band* as another example of ways to use ordinary objects as instruments.

Sabbeth, Alex. *Rubber-Band Banjos and a Java Jive Bass: Projects & Activities on the Science of Music & Sound.* Project illustrations by Laurel Aiello. New York: John Wiley & Sons, 1997.
After a chapter on sound and hearing, Sabbeth provides instructions on making stringed, wind, and percussion instruments. Explanations and background on the actual instruments are given first.
Recapitulation: Though the materials used in making these instruments were not available during Colonial days, these instruments are easy to make.

Music, Music for Everyone

Bartoletti, Susan Campbell. *Dancing with Dziadziu.* Illustrated by Annika Nelson. San Diego: Harcourt Brace, 1997.
Gabriela dances for her bedridden Polish grandmother, Babci, and listens again to her stories of dancing every Saturday night with her husband Dziadziu.
Development: Use this book to discuss one example of family traditions. The Polish dances of polka, mazurka, and polonaise are mentioned, as are the Easter foods and traditions.

Wardlaw, Lee. *Saturday Night Jamboree.* Pictures by Barry Root. New York: Dial Books for Young Readers, 2000.
A young girl doesn't mind having a babysitter when her parents go country dancing on a Saturday night because Carlene brings dress-up clothes and they sing country love songs. Chet cooks up chili for their "honky-tonk Kitchen Diner," and Uncle Buffalo Beau tells cowboy stories. When her parents stay home, they have their own jamboree.
Development: The extended family of babysitters adds a new dimension to the role of music in a family. The rhyming narrative is rhythmic and reads like a country song.

Nicholas Cricket

Florian, Douglas. "Crickets." In *Insectlopedia,* 41. San Diego: Harcourt Brace, 1998.
This six-line poem describes how a cricket "fiddles" by rubbing its wings.
Recapitulation: Add this poem to your Cricket Concert.

Livingston, Myra Cohn. "Crickets." In *Knock at a Star: A Child's Introduction to Poetry,* [compiled by] X. J. Kennedy and Dorothy M. Kennedy, illustrated by Karen Lee Baker, 106. Boston: Little, Brown, 1999.
Each line of the poem has two words, and all the words are one syllable. The poem mimics the steady rhythm of a cricket sound and is ideal for a reading by two people.
Recapitulation: Use this poem with Fleischman's "House Crickets."

Oh, A-Hunting We Will Go

Kellogg, Steven. *A-Hunting We Will Go!* New York: Morrow Junior Books, 1998.
Two children "hunt" for their stuffed animals as they get ready for bed.
Coda: Kellogg's verses can be sung to the tune in Langstaff's book. The music included is a different melody.

DANCES

Barn Dance

Boynton, Sandra. *Barnyard Dance*. New York: Workman, 1993.
This board book uses descriptive verbs that allow students to improvise a square dance just like the animals in the book. They can "twirl with the pig," "bounce with the bunny," and "slide with the sheep."
Development: Instead of learning actual square dance steps, younger students can improvise to the antic actions of this book.

McLoughland, Beverly. "Birds' Square Dance." In *Song and Dance*, poems selected by Lee Bennett Hopkins, illustrated by Cheryl Munro Taylor, 18. New York: Simon & Schuster, 1997.

The Dancing Granny

"Little Sally Water." In *Brown Girl in the Ring: An Anthology of Song Games from the Eastern Caribbean*, collected and documented by Alan Lomax, J. D. Elder, and Bess Lomax Hawes, 140-141. New York: Pantheon Books, 1997.
Development: Share with the students the various names given this song and its origins in British lore as "Little Sally Water." Instructions are given for playing a circle game while singing the song.

Merriam, Eve. *You Be Good & I'll Be Night*. Pictures by Karen Lee Schmidt. New York: Mulberry Paperback Books, 1994.
Paperback edition of the 1988 Morrow Junior Books title.

Dancing the Breeze

Gray, Libba Moore. *My Mama Had a Dancing Heart*. Illustrated by Raúl Colón. New York: Orchard Books, 1995.
A ballerina reminisces about dancing with her mother. Descriptive words, such as "tip-tapping, song-singing, finger-snapping," set the mood for the dancing done in each season.
Coda: Expand the lesson with this example of a dancing relationship with a mother.

Song and Dance. Poems selected by Lee Bennett Hopkins. Illustrated by Cheryl Munro Taylor. New York: Simon & Schuster, 1997.
Many of these poems feature dancing, from specific dances, such as square dancing, to dancing outside to the sounds and rhythms of nature.
Coda: Teach the students "When I Dance," "The Song of the Night," and "Nightdance" as examples of dancing poems.

Dinosaur Dances

OgBurn, Jacqueline K. *The Reptile Ball.* Pictures by John O'Brien. New York: Dial Books for Young Readers, 1997,
> Similar to *Dinosaur Dances*, these poems feature various reptiles dancing. The snakes do the "ssa-ssa-ssamba," the horned toads do the two-step, and the toad and frog do the reel.
> **Coda:** Incorporate this book into a lesson on reptiles. The glossary in the book defines all the reptiles mentioned. Assign a poem to the person or group investigating that reptile. Suggest that the students make stick puppets that accurately portray the reptiles' physical characteristics and use them to act out the poem.

Mirandy and Brother Wind

McKissack, Patricia C. *Mirandy and Brother Wind.* Illustrated by Jerry Pinkney. New York: Dragonfly Books, 1996.
> Paperback edition.

"That's How the Cake Walk's Done." Original Words and Music by J. Leubrie Hill. New Words Adapted by Wade Hudson. In *How Sweet the Sound: African-American Songs for Children,* selected by Wade and Cheryl Hudson, illustrated by Floyd Cooper, 17. New York: Scholastic, 1995.
> This picture book illustrates the text to African-American songs throughout history. The Hudsons include the melody lines of the songs at the end of the book and a summary of the songs' origins.
> **Recapitulation:** Play the melody and discuss the syncopation of the ragtime. The words describe how a cakewalk is done.

Shimmy Shake Earthquake: Don't Forget to Dance Poems

Song and Dance. Poems selected by Lee Bennett Hopkins. Illustrated by Cheryl Munro Taylor. New York: Simon & Schuster, 1997.
> All of the poems in the collection are about music and dance and add a lyrical dimension to the rhythmic emphasis in *Shimmy Shake Earthquake: Don't Forget to Dance Poems.*
> **Coda:** Include these poems as examples of free verse and lyrical imagery.

Skip to My Lou

Fleming, Denise. *Barnyard Banter.* New York: Henry Holt, 1994.
> Each two-page spread introduces a farm animal, its location and its sound. For example, "cows in the pasture, moo, moo, moo" and "roosters in the barnyard, cock-a-doodle-doo."
> **Coda:** This book can be sung to the tune of "Skip to My Lou."

"Skip to My Lou." Pete Seeger. In *Smithsonian Folkways Children's Music Collection.* Smithsonian Folkways Recordings, 1998. SF CD 45043. CD.

Westcott, Nadine Bernard. *Skip to My Lou.* Boston: Little, Brown, 1989, 2000.
> Board book edition.

Ziefert, Harriet. *Sleepy-O!* Illustrated by Laura Rader. Boston: Houghton Mifflin, 1997.

This illustrated folksong asks, "What'll I do with this baby-o, If she won't go to sleepy-o?" Each verse supplies a remedy. The melody line included is arranged by Jean Ritchie. She also relates her experience as a youngster going to a square dance or play-party.

Coda: Teach students the chorus to this song, so they can join in as you sing the verses. Relate the page that includes a square dance to the dance they learned for "Skip to My Lou."

HISTORY

The Boy Who Loved Music

Celenza, Anna Harwell. *The Farewell Symphony.* Illustrated by JoAnn E. Kitchel. Watertown, Mass.: Talewinds, 2000.

This retelling of the true story of the circumstances surrounding the composing of Haydn's *Farewell Symphony* includes an author's note, an explanation of the 18th-century symphony, and a CD containing Haydn's Symphony no. 31 "Hornsignal" and Symphony no. 45 "Farewell."

Development: Use this recording to identify the instruments in the last movement of the *Farewell Symphony.*

Koscielniak, Bruce. *The Story of the Incredible Orchestra: An Introduction to Musical Instruments and the Symphony Orchestra.* Boston: Houghton Mifflin, 2000.

Koscielniak provides a history of the development of the orchestra, detailing the instruments of each period and how and when they were improved. The illustrations of the instruments include numerous captions that add to the information in the text.

Development: The chapter on the Classical Age mentions Haydn and explains the "crook horns" used in the Classical orchestra. Compare the pictures of the various horns in this book and Lasker's.

Cowboy Dreams

"The Cowboy's Lament (The Streets of Laredo)." In *Gonna Sing My Head Off! American Folk Songs for Children,* collected and arranged by Kathleen Krull, illustrated by Allen Garns, 22-23. New York: Alfred A. Knopf, 1995.

"Home on the Range." In *Gonna Sing My Head Off! American Folk Songs for Children,* 50-51.

"I Ride an Old Paint." In *Gonna Sing My Head Off! American Folk Songs for Children,* 52-53.

Medearis, Angela Shelf. *The Zebra-Riding Cowboy: A Folk Song from the Old West.* Collected by Angela Shelf Medearis. Illustrated by Maria Cristina Brusca. New York: Henry Holt, 1992.

This song tells the story of a "greenhorn" who wants to borrow a horse from a cowboy camp. The cowboys, as a joke, present him with the wild Zebra Dun, but the greenhorn, despite his educated ways, is a true cowboy and tames the horse. Medearis adds another element to the story by depicting the greenhorn as a black cowboy and supplies a history of the black cowboy in an afterword. The song is included.

Exposition: *The Zebra-Riding Cowboy* uses the dotted rhythm in the melody and the accompaniment.

Coda: Use this story to include the role of the black cowboy in the history of the Old West.

"Red River Valley." In *Gonna Sing My Head Off! American Folk Songs for Children*, 85-86.

The Erie Canal

Harness, Cheryl. *The Amazing Impossible Erie Canal*. New York: Simon & Schuster Books for Young Readers, 1995.

Embellished with numerous illustrations and maps, this book recounts the reasons for the building of the Erie Canal, the story of the celebratory first journey from Buffalo, N.Y., to the Atlantic Ocean near Sandy Hook, N.J., and the significance of the canal to U.S. history.

Recapitulation: This book includes many details of the building of the canal and the boats that traveled it.

Follow the Drinking Gourd

Rappaport, Doreen. *Freedom River*. Pictures by Bryan Collier. New York: Hyperion Books for Children, 2000.

This true story recounts one of the many times that John Parker, a former slave, risked his life to help a slave family escape across the Ohio River to freedom.

Coda: Use this book as background information on the Underground Railroad. The book includes an 1847 map of the Ohio River on the endpapers and a historical note on John Parker.

Stein, R. Conrad. *The Underground Railroad*. New York: Children's Press, 1997.

This short book contains a comprehensive history of the Underground Railroad, including information on Harriet Tubman, John Parker, and the use of spirituals as coded messages for escaping. It also contains many historical photographs and advertisements.

Coda: Use for additional information on Harriet Tubman and other "conductors."

Mozart Tonight

Gatti, Anne. *The Magic Flute*. Illustrated by Peter Malone. San Francisco: Chronicle Books, 1997.

Gatti tells the story of *The Magic Flute* in short scenes. Musical highlights from each scene are on an accompanying CD.

Isadora, Rachel. *Young Mozart*. New York, Viking, 1997.

Starting with anecdotes of Mozart's early displays of genius, this picture book biography includes many highlights of Mozart's life and ends with his death.

Malam, John. *Wolfgang Amadeus Mozart*. Minneapolis: Carolrhoda Books, 1997.

This short, easy-to-read biography of Mozart includes many paintings of the Mozart family and photographs of places he lived and worked. "Important Dates" and "Keywords" are included at the back of the book.

Ragtime Tumpie

Chocolate, Debbi. *The Piano Man*. Illustrations by Eric Velasquez. New York: Walker, 1998.

Writing about her grandfather, Chocolate relates his life as a vaudeville musician and piano player for silent movies.

Recapitulation: The grandfather also played ragtime and learned from Jelly Roll Morton and Scott Joplin. This account with its striking illustrations captures the flavor of the times. It will complement the factual material.

Tate, Eleanora E. *African American Musicians*. New York: John Wiley & Sons, 2000.

African American Musicians contains short biographies in chronological order from Elizabeth Taylor Greenfield, a singer in the mid-1800s to Queen Latifah, a rap star of the 1990s. Includes a biography of Scott Joplin.

INDEX

A My Name Is Alice, 10
Absolute music, 54-55
Accelerando, 15-16
Accent, 17, 107
Accordion, 68
Adagio, 95
"All the Pretty Little Horses, 21, 22
"Allee allee in free," 80
Allegro assai, 95
Alliteration, 71
Alphabet, 3-4, 11, 81
Ananse, 79-80. *See also* Anansi
Anansi, 79-80
Andante, 95
"Animal Fair, The, 28
Armstrong, Louis, 3, 49
Art appreciation, 41-43
"At a Georgia Camp Meeting," 86, 87
"Au Clair de la Lune," 32

Baker, Josephine, 41, 107
Ball-bouncing rhymes, 10-11
Band, 62
Banjo, 70
Bass viol, 95
"Bear Went over the Mountain, The," 81, 82
Bears, 34-36, 61-63
Beats, 8
   strong, 5-6
Beethoven, Ludwig van, 54-55
Berlioz, Hector, 62
Bernstein, Leonard, vii, viii
Big Dipper, 104
Bird songs, 25-27
Birdcalls, 25-27
Birds, 25-27
Blue notes, 49
Blues, 51-53
Boogie, 88
Borders, 61-63, 69
Bugaloo, 88
"By'm Bye," 21, 22

Cacophony, 59-60
Cakewalk, 86-87
Calabash, 79-80
Canon, 44, 46-47
"Casey Jones," 15
Cassidy, Hopalong, 99
Cheers, 3-4
Chord, 44-45
   dominant (V), 51
   subdominant (IV), 51
   tonic (I), 51
Chorus, 90, 101, 103-4
Chuck-will's-widow, 26
Circle story, 37-38
Clacker, 66
Clapping rhymes, 11
Classical music, 54
Classical period, 95-97, 105-6
Claves, 66-99
Clavichord, 105
Clef, 37
Coda, vii
Color—in art and music, 43
Colors, 30-31
Common meter. *See* Meter: common
Compound duple meter. *See* Meter: compound duple
Conga, 83, 85
Corncob whistle, 66
Counting, 34-36
Counting-out rhyme, 10, 16
Cowboys, 98-100
"Cowboy's Lament, The," 98
"Crawdad Song," 28
Cricket Concert, 71
Crickets, 70-71
Crocodiles, 8-9

Dactyl, 15-16
Debussy, Claude, 86
Development—in Sonata-allegro movement, vii
dinosaurs, 83-85
Do—definition in solmization, 23

127

"Do Re Mi," 104
Don Giovanni, 105
Do-si-do, 77
"Draw a Bucket of Water," 37, 38. *See also* "Sugar Bowl"
Duet, 46
Duncan, Isadora, 41
Duple meter. *See* Meter: duple
Dynamic signs, 59-60

Eighth note, 16, 81
Embouchure, 72
Emphasis, 46
Encore, 62
"Engine, engine number nine," 16
Ensemble, 46
Ensemble playing, 46-47
Erie Canal, 101-2
"Erie Canal, The," 101. *See also* "Low Bridge! Everybody Down"
Exposition—in Sonata-allegro movement, vii

Family Music Fest, 69
Fandango, 88
Farewell Symphony (Haydn), 96
Fiddle-I-Fee, 23-24. *See also* "I Bought Me a Cat"
Fifth. *See* Interval: fifth
Fitzgerald, Ella, 3
Fleischman, Paul, vii, viii
Flowers, 81-82
Folk song, 103
"Follow the Drinking Gourd," 103, 104
Forte, 59
Fortissimo, 59
4/4 meter. *See* Meter: common
French horn, 73
"Frère Jacques," 45

Gershwin, George, 41-43
Glissando, 59-60
Glockenspiel, 30
Golliwog, 86-87
"Golliwog's Cakewalk," 86, 87
"Goodbye Old Paint," 98, 100
Grandfathers, 25-27
Grandmothers, 28-29
Guiro, 66

Half note, 16
Handy, W. C., 53
Harmonic pattern—12-bar blues, 51-53
Harmonica, 26
Harmony, 94-95
Haydn, Franz Joseph, 95-97
"Hickory Dickory Dock," 5-7
Hoedown, 77
"Home on the Range," 98
Home tone. *See* Keynote
Horn, 73, 95
Hunting horn, 72
"Hush, Little Baby," 25, 27

"I Bought Me a Cat," 23. *See also Fiddle-I-Fee*
Idiophone, 59-60
"I'm a Poor Lonesome Cowboy," 98
Improvisation, 3-4
"Inchworm," 103, 104
Inflection, 46
Insects, 46-47, 70-71
Instruments
  folk, 66
  homemade, 28-29, 48-50, 59-60, 66-67
Interval
  fifth, 21
  third, 45

Jazz, 48-49
"Jennie Jenkins," 30
"John Henry," 15
Joplin, Scott, 107-8
Jug band, 50
"Jumping jack" doll, 67

Kazoo, 70, 72
Key, 54
  major, 22, 101
  minor, 101
Keynote, 37-38
Kodaly hand signs, 34-35

Largo, 62
Limerick, 5-7
Lindy, 88

"Listen to the Mockingbird," 25, 27
Listening, 64-65
"Little Sally Walker," 79, 80
Lone Ranger, 99
"Low Bridge! Everybody Down," 101. *See also* "Erie Canal, The"
Lullaby, 21-22

Magic Flute, The, 105, 106
"Mama Don't Allow," 48, 49. *See also* "Mammy Don't 'Low"
"Mammy Don't 'Low," 48. *See also* "Mama Don't Allow"
"Man on the Flying Trapeze, The," 83, 84
"Mary Mack," 10. *See also* "Miss Mary Mack"
"Mary Wore a Red Dress," 30
Matisse, Henri, 41-43
Measure, 8, 83
Melodic patterns, 23
   bird songs, 25
   G-E-A-G-E, 79-80. *See also* Teasing chant
   mi-re-do, 24
   mi-sol, 24
   sol-mi, 36
   sol-mi-do, 36
   three descending notes, 45
Menuet, 95
Meter, 5, 83-84
   common, 8
   compound duple, 5-7
   duple, 5
Metronome, 8
Mezzo forte, 59
Mezzo piano, 59
Mi—definition in solmization, 23
Mice, 5-7, 44-45
Mime, 32
Minute. *See* Menuet
"Miss Mary Mack," 10. *See also* "Mary Mack"
Mnemonics, 103-4
Mockingbirds, 25-27
Mouth sounds, 48-50
Movement, 81-82
   through poetry, 88-89
Movement—symphonic, 95
Mozart, Wolfgang Amadeus, 105-6
"Mulberry Bush, The," 5, 32, 33
Musicians—treatment in eighteenth century, 95-97, 105-6

"Name Game, The," 3, 4
"Noble Duke of York, The," 83, 84

"O, The Train's off the Track," 15, 17. *See also* "Train's off the Track"
Octave, 21
"Old Joe Clarke," 77, 78
"Old MacDonald Had a Farm," 23, 24, 37, 38
"On Top of Old Smoky," 28
Onomatopoeia, 8-9, 64-65
Opera, 105
Oppossums, 12-14
Orchestra, 61-63
   sections, 62, 63
Ostinato, 12-13
Overtones, 72, 79
Overture, 105

Pace, 46
Paint horse, 99
Pantomime, 32-33
Pentatonic scale. *See* Scale: pentatonic
Phrase, vii, 90
Pianissimo, 59
Piano—dynamic sign, 59
Pianoforte, 105
Picasso, Pablo, 41-43
Pierrot, 32-33
Pitch, 3-4, 45
   matching, 29, 31
Play party, 90-91
Polka, 83
Polonaise, 88
Post horn, 72
Pourquoi story, 12-13
Presto, 96
Prodigy, 105
Program music, 54-55
Puppet show, 13

Quarter note, 16, 81

Ragtime music, 87, 107-9
Rainey, "Ma," 53
Rap, 51
Re—definition in solmization, 23
Readers theatre, 12-13, 80
Recapitulation—in Sonata-allegro movement, vii
"Red River Valley," 98
Remington, Frederic, 98-100
Refrain, 12
Requiem, 46
Reveille, 72

Rhymes
   ball-bouncing, 10-11
   counting-out, 10, 16
Rhythm instruments, 3-4, 9, 65
Rhythmic patterns, 24
   dotted-eighth/sixteenth note, 99
"Rock-a-bye Baby," 21
"Roll Over," 34, 37, 38. *See also* "Ten in a Bed"
Rondo, 54-55
Round, 44-45
Russell, Charles M., 98-100

"St. Louis Blues," 51, 53
Salon, 42
Satie, Erik, 41-43
Scale, 21
   descending minor, 22
   E-minor, 102
   G-major, 102
   major, 21
   minor, 21
   pentatonic, 30-31
Scat singing, 3-4, 49
Sendak, Maurice, vii, viii
Serenade, 46
"Shake It to the East," 79, 80
"Shake My Sillies Out," 88, 89
Shape, 43
Sheet music covers, 107, 109
"She'll Be Comin' Round the Mountain," 28
"Skip to My Lou," 90, 91. *See also* "Skip to My Lou"
"Skip-a to My Lou," 90
Smith, Bessie, 53
Solmization, 23, 34-36
Sonata, 105
Sonata form, vii. *See also* Sonata-allegro form
Sonata-allegro form, vii
Square dances, 77-78, 91
Square-dance music, 78
Stein, Gertrude, 42
Sticks, 66
Street rhymes, 10
"Streets of Laredo." *See* "Cowboy's Lament, The"
"Sugar Bowl," 37, 38. *See also* "Draw a Bucket of Water"

Symphony, 95-97, 105
Syncopation, 107-9

Tall tales, 17
Tango, 83
Teasing chant, 79. *See also* Melodic patterns: G-E-A-G-E
Tempo, 46
Tempo indicators, 95-97
"Ten in a Bed," 34. *See also* "Roll Over"
Texture, 43
Thomson, Virgil, 42
"Three Blind Mice," 44, 45
"Three Myopic Rodents," 44
Time signatures
   4/4, 83
   3/4, 83
Tonality, 37-38
Trains, 15-17
"Train's off the Track," 15. *See also* "O, The Train's off the Track"
Treble clef, 37
Triad, 44
   broken, 34, 36
Trickster stories, 79-80
Trochee, 8, 15-16
Tub thumper, 66
"Turkey in the Straw," 77, 78
12-bar blues, 51-52

Underground Railroad, 103-4

Verse, 90, 101, 103-4
Voice, 64
Voices—in poetry and music, 46-47

Waltz, 83
Washboard, 28
Washtub bass. *See* Tub thumper
Western painting, 98-100
"William Tell Overture," 98, 99
Wind, 81-82, 86-87

ABOUT THE AUTHOR

Donna B. Levene

Since childhood, Donna B. Levene has had a dual interest in music and libraries. She pursued this interest in college by obtaining a Bachelor of Fine Arts degree in Piano Performance at the University of Wisconsin—Milwaukee while working part-time in the music library of Schaum Music Publishing Company. She then attended the University of Denver and received a Masters in Library Science. After graduating she worked as a professional librarian in the Architecture and Fine Arts Library at the University of Florida and Perkins Library at Duke University. Ms. Levene acquired a teaching certificate and media endorsement in Colorado while teaching piano in her home and currently is Library Media Specialist at Homestead Elementary in Englewood, Colorado. She lives in Aurora, Colorado, with her husband, Barry, and two sons, Nathan and Alex. Her hobbies include playing the piano, folk dancing, and bird watching.

from *Teacher Ideas Press*

GLUES, BREWS, AND GOOS
Recipes and Formulas for Almost Any Classroom Project
Diana F. Marks

You've got to have it! This indispensable activity book pulls together hundreds of practical, easy recipes and formulas for classroom projects. From paints and salt map mixtures to volcanic action formulas, these kid-tested projects make learning authentic and enjoyable. All projects use ingredients that are easy to find and processes that are up-to-date. **Grades K–6.**
xvi, 179p. 8½x11 paper ISBN 1-56308-362-0

SCIENCE THROUGH CHILDREN'S LITERATURE, 2d Edition
Carol M. Butzow and John W. Butzow

The Butzows' groundbreaking, critically acclaimed, and best-selling resource has been thoroughly revised and updated with new titles and new activities for today's classroom. More than 30 exciting instructional units integrate all areas of the curriculum and serve as models to educators at all levels. Adopted as a supplementary text in schools of education nationwide, this resource features outstanding children's fiction books that are rich in scientific concepts yet equally well known for their strong story lines and universal appeal. **Grades K–3.**
xix, 205p. 8½x11 paper ISBN 1-56308-651-4

MULTICULTURAL FOLKTALES
Readers Theatre for Elementary Students
Suzanne I. Barchers

Introduce your students to other countries and cultures through these engaging readers theatre scripts based upon traditional folk and fairy tales. Representing more than 30 countries and regions, the 40 reproducible scripts are accompanied by presentation suggestions and recommendations for props and delivery. **Grades 1–5.**
xxi, 188p. 8½x11 paper ISBN 1-56308-760-X

SUPER SIMPLE STORYTELLING
A Can-Do Guide for Every Classroom, Every Day
Kendall Haven

Aside from guides to more than 40 powerful storytelling exercises, you'll find the Golden List of what an audience really needs from storytelling, a proven, step-by-step system for successfully learning and remembering a story, and the Great-Amazing-Never-Fail Safety Net to prevent storytelling disasters. This system has been successfully used by more than 15,000 educators across the country. **All Levels.**
xxvii, 229p. 8½x11 paper ISBN 1-56308-681-6

MORE SOCIAL STUDIES THROUGH CHILDREN'S LITERATURE
An Integrated Approach
Anthony D. Fredericks

These dynamic literature-based activities will help you energize the social studies curriculum and implement national and state standards. Each of these 33 units offers book summaries, social studies topic areas, critical thinking questions, and dozens of easy-to-do activities for every grade level. The author also gives practical guidelines for integrating literature across the curriculum, lists of Web sites useful in social studies classes, and annotated bibliographies of related resources. **Grades K–5.**
xix, 225p. 8½x11 paper ISBN 1-56308-761-8

For a free catalog or to place an order, please contact:
Teacher Ideas Press • Dept. B050 • P.O. Box 6633 • Englewood, CO • 80155-6633
800-237-6124 • www.lu.com/tip • Fax: 303-220-8843